Connect
to
Influence

Connect to Influence

Leveraging Relationships
for a Lifetime of Career Success

Connect to Influence: Leveraging Relationships for a
Lifetime of Career Success

Copyright © 2017
Allison K. Summers

Publisher
Come Into Your OWN Publishing, a subsidiary of
Business Over Coffee International (BOCI)
5865 Ridgeway Center Pkwy Ste 300
Memphis, Tennessee 38120
www.comeintoyourown.com
info@comeintoyourown.com

Come Into Your

Own

Edited by Bethany Sledge

First edition: April 2017

Contents

"I always say:
Don't make plans; make options."

—Jennifer Aniston, actress, producer,
philanthropist, forever a friend to all

Foreword

I have always avoided networking like the plague; it always felt a little invasive to me. I hated attending events where people would come up to me, thrust a business card into my hand, and try to sell me services I had neither need of nor desire for. I was always worried that people would think the same of me. For years I was never very good at tapping into my own network or asking for help when I needed it, although my last two jobs came from within my network. I was more reactive than proactive, responding to opportunities presented or requests made.

That all changed when I met Allison. I connected with her through LinkedIn, and I just happened to add a line to the connection request, saying, "If you need anything, just ask. I know many people write that, but I really do mean it."

To my surprise, Allison immediately jumped at the offer and requested a Skype call. We talked for well over an hour, sharing our thoughts on many things, including authoring a book. Having written four books myself, I was more than happy to share my insights, to offer to connect Allison to my publishers, and even to proofread the book.

In that moment of connection, our networks intertwined and our collective influence increased significantly. In return for the favor offered, Allison introduced me to the CEO of an event-planning company, who organizes over nine thousand events per year. For my occupation as a speaker, this was an excellent connection, and not only did she introduce me, but she recommended me, which gave the connection significantly more value.

As I got involved in the project, Allison taught me that not only was networking not a dirty word, but she also taught me techniques which I have put into practice, helping me to increase my speaking and consulting practice. Before, less than 50 percent of my work came from within my network; now it is closer to 90 percent. Making sales calls can be tough—daunting, even—but it's considerably easier when you are speaking with someone you know or to whom you have been recommended.

I love this book; I think it is an invaluable tool. Not only does it talk about the importance of networking, but it offers practical advice on how to go about it. Allison has a great perspective, too; not only as a great networker but as a chief executive officer she offers insights into how C-suite people think and the demands they face, which helps us to grasp how we can approach them and offer the right service.

If you learn these techniques and apply them, they will open many opportunities that would otherwise not be available to you. Why live an ordinary life when you can build an influential network and live an extraordinary one?

It's never too late to start, but the sooner you start to build and work your network, the quicker the great opportunities will present themselves.

—Gordon Tredgold

One of *Inc.*'s Top 100 leadership and management experts, author, international keynote speaker, #2 on the Top 15 Must-Read Leadership Blogs, #19 Top Social Media Marketing Influencer according to *CEOWorld*, and a contributing author for *Inc.*, *Entrepreneur*, and the Huffington Post.

1

Connections Change Everything

How you choose to play the world is completely up to you. There are stories all around us of the underdog who makes it big; of people who successfully learn to 'fail up'; of those who begin their life's journey with the most underprivileged circumstance, a debilitating physical challenge, or sad, sad story only to fight their way to the top. And then there's my favorite category, the people who make up their minds to reinvent themselves and not let their past define who they will be in the future.

People who choose to play larger in life have one significant trait in common—they think beyond the space they currently occupy. These winners know that the actions they take today will help to set them up for a better tomorrow.

If you want to be irreplaceable, you must always be different. —*J. T. Foxx, World's #1 wealth coach and a firm believer that while you may start unknown, you should finish unforgettable*

The world's most highly successful entrepreneurs and business leaders know that the best way to expand the space you occupy is by developing and leveraging relevant human connections with people of diverse backgrounds, professions, cultures, and a significantly higher economic standing and level of influence. So, I state again: ***How you choose to play the world is completely up to you***.

You can choose to play small or play larger than life. You choose to be the success story. Why choose a hard life of submitting to the views and limitations that others define and are so happy to thrust upon you? Why not embrace the game, set your mind, and focus to do more and be more?

Connections improve who we are and what we become in the world. They introduce us to new ideas, link us to more people, and provide greater options for forward momentum. Without connections, you will likely become stranded, outdated, and obsolete.

You can do what everyone else does and choose to sit back and wait for opportunities to find you, or you can resolve to establish a 'connective mind-set' and work to occupy a larger space in the world through building a vibrant network of connections.

What are the rewards of such efforts? Building a bold network will allow you to:

+ Reshape how you think
+ Extend knowledge
+ Tap shortcuts to resources
+ Benchmark for excellence
+ Sharpen your business acumen
+ Frame new business perspectives
+ Gain competitive insights
+ Attract new business opportunities
+ Transform your behaviors to match the expert leaders
+ Polish your professional presence
+ Develop periscope abilities to see ahead and around corners
+ Accelerate your success
+ Elevate your brand equity in the marketplace

So why this book? What makes it different? I kept three main principles in mind as I wrote this book for you.

1. To help you construct your 'WHY' for the purpose behind connecting. To be driven to success, you must see this as an indispensable mission and not just as an 'I know I should do it' that you think of every now and then.

2. To know that growing your network quickly and vastly is probable if you know the secrets and insights to become a super connector.

3. To gain insights into the human side of connecting so you can be more authentic, relatable, and efficient.

Connections help move you from where you are to where you want to be. I have a phrase that I always share with my teams, "You can't get better staying within the four walls of the office." So are you ready to get out and be better?

Fantastic! Forward we go. . . .

2

Will You Be Lost or Found?
In or Out? Rich or Poor?

I know you are thinking, *You got me excited about connecting, and now you are going to be a downer.* Yes, this chapter is the reality check you need to help develop your 'WHY' and to understand the importance of your mission.

Business is changing. Work of the future will not look like the work of today. The employment models of the recent past are quickly fading and new models are rising. Job security is not a phrase spoken any more because it simply does not exist. Sadly, when the pendulum swings in the modern-day business economy, there is little true security.

As we outsource and offshore more and more work, the good opportunities that used to be available are starting to diminish. As the competition grows with the largest generation (hello, Millennials) flowing into the workforce and the pool of available jobs shrinking, this will only make it harder for people to find their dream jobs or any jobs.

"Surely you don't mean *me*?" It is true there is a 'war for talent,' and you can say to yourself, "I have a degree, experience, and skills." But while a great education is fine, it's no guarantee of a good job as 48 percent of employed college graduates hold positions that don't require a four-year degree, much less the degree they hold.

Identifying the perfect talent at exactly the moment I need it is incredibly difficult. I can tell you that as a business leader 1) I probably won't be able to find you right when I need you, or 2) if I do find you, I may not be able to deftly determine that you are as 'shiny and attractive' as you find yourself to be.

Although it varies between companies and the job type, on average 250 resumes are received for each corporate job opening. That means your chances of landing that job is 250 to one!

And today, the first pass of your resume or CV may not even go past human eyes. Much of the initial resume screening is performed by automated tracking systems (ATS) which reject 75 percent of the candidates. Many potentially qualified candidates are rejected because their resumes did not have the right formatting or the particular keywords that the ATS was looking for.

If you make it as one of the 25 percent that is not rejected, you go on to be assessed by a live recruiter. However, you may be shocked to know that the average recruiter spends a mere six seconds reviewing a resume . . . which doesn't really give you much of an opportunity to stand out.

But even if you do get through all of that and land your dream job, it's still not 'smooth sailing' because, according to the US Bureau of Labor Statistics, the average worker will hold ten different jobs before age forty. And sadly, this number is projected to grow.

So even if you're lucky enough to win the application lottery, you need to recognize that you are going to have to repeat this process between ten and twenty times during your career. Does the sound of that excite you?

And while you are thinking about that, consider this next somber fact. If you get laid off or find yourself out of work, the average length of time to find a new job is 27.2

weeks! Is this the type of game you want to have played with your life?

But the situation on the side of the organization is not much better than it is for the candidate. The pressure on business leaders to get a new hire's skills and culture match right is immense because in business today, organizations already run teams short on people power.

Because of this, we hiring executives want—no, we need—an employee who can walk in the door and do absolutely everything on our three-page job description because we no longer have time to take the wonderful person with only 50 percent of the skills and train him or her on the other 50 percent. The pressure of getting 'the hire' right is also compounded by the fact that the moment a company takes someone on as a full-time employee, the risks for litigation stemming from a dismissal or separation is incredibly high.

But let's be really honest, may we? Think of the infrastructure a company must maintain to support one full-time equivalent (FTE): salary, fringe, technology, resources, development, and more. Fringe is all the employer-paid taxes and benefits that come along with your salary. Once upon a time in a workplace long ago, the phrase 'fringe benefits' meant you were getting something really special—like a key to the executive washroom. Today it is a luxury if you get both medical and dental insurance, and if an employer throws in vision insurance, well, that is just downright crazy.

The fringe on a regular employee salary can be anywhere from 35 to 50 percent on top of base salary. When you add infrastructure—square footage, desks, computers, phones, utilities, insurance, etc.—the cost of supporting one FTE is downright scary. Let's face it, the key to the executive washroom in your future may very well be for the bathroom in your own home as you may need to be an independent contractor or business operator in your own right.

The truth is: If you don't begin to think about your career and business life differently, you will be ousted to the outskirts of the shadow economy. And once you go to the shadows, you may never be seen or heard from again.

Say good-bye to asking for a six-figure income, to becoming a highly compensated employee, and to bolstering that retirement account that guarantees your financial freedom one day. The shadow economy has swallowed many souls, and it is poised to take many more who are not careful to work today to protect their income of tomorrow. You must rise above the views of business taught to you by your parents, universities, or coworkers as those views will never open the business world to you in the ways that you both want it and need it.

We can create the ultimate job security by becoming less dependent on the organization for which we work and more dependent on our own resources. —Bo Bennett, entrepreneur, tech mogul, author, and testament to the fact that you must have control over your odds of achieving success

---

The words 'free, fast, and mass' are very frightening to many long-standing businesses. These words represent how the rise of technology has marginalized the value of many goods and services being offered today. He with the best technology often wins, and massive conglomerates and big-box mentality can eat up the individual and smaller entities.

'Disrupters' accomplish what no one could have conceived only months before and force old models to falter and new models to rise. Whether cloaked as Business 4.0 or the Fourth Industrial Revolution, no one can deny the impact of rapidly changing technology and redefined societal norms and needs.

It's not all doom and gloom. You must view yourself as your own business venture. You need to become an expert in the trade of you; you need to build influence. You must be determined to have brand attributes that people are willing to buy into, or they will happily look you over and get their needs met elsewhere. Not only must you work your way up the proverbial corporate ladder swiftly and powerfully, but you must at the same time learn entrepreneurial skills and consider maintaining a side business so, when organizations fail you, you have a safety net to carry you along.

More than ever the world needs small businesses and independent contractors to fill the gaps in needs. I predict another significant rise in people working for themselves, a renaissance of the global workforce becoming agents of free trade. In much of the world, corporations seek to squeeze margins and feel a greater pinch of taxation and the weight of carrying employee benefits. Companies and individuals who can relieve stress and provide solutions will be valuable part-ners to business, governments, and NGO's.

And as you operate your own business venture, people and companies must be able to find you in their time of need. The only way to ensure that happens is you must prepare to be a highly influential and connected individual in both the hu-man realm and the digital one.

You must recognize that your connections in life, in terms of both quality and quantity, will serve as a predictor of your future success.

Takeaways

☐ There is a war for talent, and many talented people are casualties of that war.

Connect to Influence

☐ You need to look at your career differently and take a new approach.
☐ It is up to the individual to figure out how he/she can maintain a sustainable, competitive advantage that will help drive his/her own personal economy.

References:

Most frequently outsourced work.
http://www.cheatsheet.com/breaking-news/the-12-most-frequently-outsourced-business-tasks.html/

48 percent of college graduates work in jobs that require no degree.
http://www.forbes.com/sites/susanadams/2013/05/28/half-of-college-grads-are-working-jobs-that-don't-require-a-degree/#415671a910bb

Average of 250 resumes.
https://www.eremedia.com/ere/why-you-cant-get-a-job-recruiting-explained-by-the-numbers/

75 percent of resumes are rejected by Automated Tracking Systems, ATS, which are used by most corporations.
http://www.cio.com/article/2398753/careers-staffing/5-insider-secrets-for-beating-applicant-tracking-systems.html

Unemployment duration, October 2016, average 27.2 wks.
http://www.deptofnumbers.com/unemployment/duration/

3

What Is Influence?

T he dictionary definition of influence is as follows:

> *Influence is the effect that a person or thing has on someone's decisions, opinions, or behavior or on the way something happens.*

Why is influence important? Why must you think of it as you develop your strategy to make new, impactful connections?

When we lack influence, we are powerless. We have limited ability to shape our future or obtain the outcomes that we would like to have or feel that we deserve. We are left to float on the sea, going whichever way the economic winds or political currents take us.

Life isn't fair, and we don't always get what we deserve. This is why influence is important, and the more we have, the more control we have over our future. As our influence increases so does the number of opportunities that will be available to us, as well as our chances of landing them.

Think about someone who has influence over you. Think about how that one person can impact your thought processes, your decision-making, and even your actions. If you have a difficult problem or challenge, do you seek that individual out and ask for his or her advice and input? I know that I do.

21

If you had an opportunity and you needed someone you could trust to do the job, would you go to the market and take potluck, or would you look for someone you already know and trust? Given that 85 percent of vacancies are filled through networking, I think the answer to that one is clear.

Influence is a key to a door that won't open for everyone. So where does our influence come from? There are five sources of influence:

♦ Your position
♦ Your knowledge and expertise
♦ Your character
♦ Your reputation
♦ Your network

Position

Position is the role that you occupy, and with that comes a pre-defined level of influence. Reflect on the difference in influence between the CEO of a major corporation and the janitor of the same company. Even without knowing the two individuals, you would have a different opinion of them and any information they could provide to you simply based on the job title.

Many people would treat each of them differently and respond to requests from each one differently. Some positions clearly come with built-in respect, and that can certainly work in your favor.

But that kind of influence is only temporary and is usually only available when you occupy the position. An out-of-work CEO carries less influence than one currently in the role, but there is always some residual influence associated with roles that you have occupied. Like a good degree, no one can take away the knowledge you earned in positions that you have held. Which leads to the next point. . . .

Knowledge and Expertise

Knowledge and expertise relate to the assets you bring to the table regarding your education, skills, abilities, and life experience. The more valuable and rare these assets are, the more influence and opportunity you will have.

Consider when the dot-com industry first exploded; the business world couldn't identify and hire experienced people fast enough, so much so that these talented people wrote themselves their own paychecks. As the global markets become more intertwined, those who have international perspectives, speak multiple languages, and understand how to conduct business across borders will be highly sought after and respected for their knowledge and expertise. Investment in these areas gains interest exponentially.

Character

Character is about who you are as a person and how you show up in the world: how trustworthy you are, how authentically you communicate, how you treat and interact with people, and if your integrity is beyond reproach. Character leaves an impression on people which impacts the way that they view you and the level of influence that they permit you to have over them.

Simply put, character counts. If people do not trust you, this will seriously impact the level of influence you have over them. Examples of this are prevalent in famous stories of public figures gone bad. For example, you only need to look at sports to see how character issues can sideline even the most talented of players and celebrated athletes.

Be sure that whatever industry you are in, your character will be evaluated. An engaging personality cannot mask a lack of integrity.

Reputation

Reputation is what people say about you when you're not present. It's about the successes you have attained, the milestones you have achieved, and how you are known for these in the business world.

The more successful you have been, the more influence you will have as people always want to listen to or are looking for someone who has been there, seen it, done it, and crushed it.

When you have a track record of success, people see it as minimizing risks in working with you and maximizing the potential for good things to happen. When people seek you out, you have their full attention.

Network

Network is about your connections: the people you know and the resources you have access to. Your network is your force multiplier to open doors and stir up opportunities. It serves as a safety net of people whom you can call on in your time of need. It offers insight and information that you can harness to deliver a solid, competitive advantage.

With the first four areas of influence, there are limits to what we can achieve, but with a robust network, our potential is practically unlimited. By consciously adding people to our network or purposefully connecting to newer, larger networks, we remain dynamic and stand in a position of increased power.

Building a great personal brand plus activating great connections is critical whether you are rushing up the path toward an executive office, building a life as an independent contractor, or unleashing the entrepreneur in you and birthing your own brilliant business.

Knowledge, character, and reputation serve as the cornerstones of your personal brand. These attributes combined with the strength of your professional network will decide the opportunities that you will be given and the positions that you will attain. To do well in each of these areas will extend the reach and impact of the influence that you have in your own life and in the lives of others.

Influence Will Lead to Career Success

According to one research study, only one out of every 152 applicants is hired, whereas for people who are referred, the odds increase to one in 16 referrals. Do the math; this is a 600 percent improvement. I proved this true in personal experience. In the last twenty-five years of my career, I have only had to proactively seek a new position one time. Every other opportunity found me through network referrals.

In fact, character and reputation count for so much that the one time where I was 'mutually separated' from a position (it was after the birth of my second child, and frankly, I just couldn't keep up), the general manager who let me go eventually referred and set me up for an even bigger and better role with another firm. Who would have thought that the person who dismissed me would still care enough to help me move to a better situation? If you don't think everyone in your network deserves being treated with respect, come back to this story. This is when I came to fully understand: burn no bridges, hold no ill will, only look toward a better tomorrow.

A Bonus Thought on Influence . . .

When you sprinkle positivity into your personal character, your influence levels spike ever higher. Be a person whom others like to be around.

Network continually—85 percent of all jobs are filled through contacts and personal references. *—Brian Tracy, prolific author and business advisor encouraging everyone to 'Earn What You're Worth' (although I still find his advice to 'Eat that Frog!' a little unnerving)*

Takeaways

- ☐ Influence is the key to building success in your career or business life.
- ☐ You need to build a strong personal brand and a powerful network to increase your influence.
- ☐ 85 percent of vacancies are filled by networking.

References:

Definition of influence.
http://www.macmillandictionary.com/us/dictionary/american/influence_1

85 percent of vacancies are filled by referrals.
https://www.linkedin.com/pulse/new-survey-reveals-85-all-jobs-filled-via-networking-lou-adler

4

Reflect Success

When you hear the words, 'ultimate driving machine,' your experiences tell you to think about a sleek BMW hug-ging the curves of some gorgeous mountain vista road. And the phrase 'think different' will inspire visions of a little white apple stamped on both high-tech products and the hearts of fast-forward generations.

Your personal brand is what people say about you when you are not in the room—remember that. —Chris Drucker, constructor of the "Youprenuer" movement and promoter of virtual freedom (FYI, the right connections will help you order up some of that!)

In today's world we are all programmed so that any time we hear the name of a person, object, or company it will trigger emotions, perceptions, promises, and expectations within us. And your personal brand is no different. People will both talk and think about you in terms of what they believe you can deliver.

So if your personal brand is what people say about you when you're not in the room, what are you doing to mold and manage these impressions?

It is important that your brand name is always perceived positively and reflects what you want to be known for. Your persona needs to be a brand that demonstrates the value you bring and the authenticity you hold and—*this is critical*—that inspires trust. You must have a brand people will want to introduce to and share with others. If you can achieve this, your fans will help build your network in your absence.

What is your brand, and what does it say about you? Do you know? If you don't know, there is a good chance your brand is an accidental brand. An accidental brand is one that has not been crafted to portray you in your best light or to highlight all of your best talents. It's a brand that has been put together by people based on their interactions with you, their knowledge of you, and what they heard others say about you.

Now, an accidental brand is not fatal. But it probably will not represent you in exactly the way you would like to be seen or for those things you would like to be known for. An accidental brand likely will do little to attract the right people and opportunities that will increase your income potential.

But by taking control of your brand and making it intentional rather than accidental, you can look to improve and influence how you will be perceived by others. Why is this important? Because if your brand portrays you as something that you are not or that you don't want to be known for, this could keep you in a holding pattern, severely limit your opportunities, or even worse, present opportunities that you are not really interested in but you take them anyway because you feel like they represent your only options.

Consider actors. They try to do everything in their power so that they don't become typecast because when this happens it can seriously restrict the roles for which they will be considered. Actors focus on moving their brands forward, evolving and elevating themselves, and making sure that people know who they are.

Consider the American actor Tom Hanks. His first TV series role was playing a man who would dress as a woman so he could live in a cheap all-woman hotel; it was called *Bosom Buddies*. Not exactly a role that you would think would lead to a career of multiple Oscar nominations and wins. But Tom Hanks navigated his career, using each step to move ahead from TV comedy to big-screen comedy and then from big-screen comedy to big-screen drama. And while it wasn't all good (think *Joe Versus the Volcano*), with persistence he crafted his personal brand and moved from being over the top, big, and loud to being understated, immensely authentic, and believable, which delivered him recognized success for roles like *Forrest Gump*.

If it wasn't hard, everyone would do it. It's the hard that makes it great. —*Tom Hanks, inspirational legend to chocolate lovers, space enthusiasts, and human rights activists, who also knows a thing or two about acting and awards*

What Is Your Starting Point?

The first thing that you need to do is to understand your current brand attributes. To do that you need to build up a picture of what people currently think of you. You can do this in a number of ways.

- If you have testimonials or references from people on LinkedIn (or another social site) you could review those and note common recurring themes.
- Ask friends and colleagues for their perception of your brand. What do they see as your strengths, your weaknesses, and your best assets?

- Put a post on Facebook and tell people that you're trying to understand what your personal brand is and ask them to list three to five words that they associate with you.
- Contact a prior boss or coworker or look at past performance reviews to gain insight into how others have viewed your past work. Do not be defensive on the negatives; acknowledge them as real and as something you may need to address.

In order to construct a true picture of your brand as it stands today, you also need to include some people who may not be your close friends. This is because you want to understand what your 'real' brand is, not just some sugarcoated version. It is like doing a 360-degree review. If you have ever completed one of those, you know it can give great insights into your brand. You can share a similar review template with your boss, your colleagues, your teams, your suppliers, and even your customers, and they will provide input about you that gets collated into a report. If you distribute it over a simple survey tool like Survey Monkey, it can be done anonymously, which tends to lead to more accurate answers and can inform you what people really think about your skills, values, attitude, aptitude, and more.

Compile Your Data

Once you have done your research you need to take some time to evaluate it. List all the qualities that people responded as representing what you are known for today. This is what makes up your current perceived brand attributes.

The chart on the following page offers a helpful method of collecting the information you need to evaluate your brand.

How Others Perceive Your Qualities and Attributes	Desirable Yes or No?

For each of the attributes listed, indicate whether it's a quality you are happy to be associated with or not, based on how you wish to be thought of in the world. For example, if multiple people define you as caring and you're a nurse, that may be great, but if you want to be taken seriously as a business leader, being seen as caring could weaken your chances to be viewed as leader capable of making tough decisions.

Take some time to understand each quality listed and ask yourself, what is it that you do that gives people that impression of you? How are you showing up in interactions? Are these qualities consistent or inconsistent with the brand that you want to be known for? Are there behaviors you may need to stop or behaviors you must adopt in order for people to view you differently?

Stand out, or don't bother. *—Sally Hogshead, creator of the Fascination Personality Test, believer that you have no longer than the attention span of a goldfish to make a positive impression*

Taking Ownership of Your Brand Attributes

It is unlikely that your accidental brand will be one that you are perfectly happy with. I know I wasn't when I first did this. I am sure there will be some traits that shine through that you are proud of and others that you won't like hearing about. And there may even be some qualities not mentioned that you think are your best traits but haven't made the list because others don't see you the way that you see you. And that's okay, because you need to know where you stand in order to make big strides forward.

You need to take ownership of your brand, seek to make it intentional, and give people an impression that reflects who you wish to be recognized as because ultimately like attracts like and quality attracts quality. And you want to be thought of in the quality column.

Think about people whom you admire or who have something that you don't have but would like to. Include business leaders, industry experts, corporate decision makers, innovators, successful entrepreneurs, and philanthropists. What element of their personal brands are attractive to you?

Now, let's work to define the brand identity that you would like to be known for. List below a maximum of ten values, skills, and qualities that you would like others to recognize in you.

Desired Values/ Qualities/ Skills You Want to Be Known For

Here are examples to give you some ideas:

Able	Dependable	Managing
Achiever	Determined	Motivator
Accurate	Direct	Observant
Ambitious	Doer	Organized
Analytical	Dynamic	People-focused
Approachable	Easy	Polished
Author	Eloquent	Principled
Authority	Energetic	Process-driven
Balanced	Enjoyable	Profit-minded
Brave	Fast	Prompt
Business smart	Financially sound	Respecting
Clever	Friendly	Resourceful
Confident	Impeccable	Results-oriented
Competent	Innovative	Self-motivated
Completer	Intelligent	Stable
Creative	Intuitive	Strategic
Data-driven	Investigative	Successful
Decisive	Leader	Systematic

Tactful	Team-minded	Tough
Talented	Technical	Trustworthy

Compare the lists to see similarities, gaps, and discrepancies.

Desired Qualities	Perceived Qualities

Once again, think about what qualities, skills, and knowledge you may need to propel yourself forward and attract the right opportunities. Circle the top three desired qualities you need to work on and mark out those that may have gotten you where you are today but may not be needed tomorrow.

The Law of Consistency: A brand is not built overnight. Success is measured in decades, not years. —from the 22 Immutable Laws of Branding *by Al Reis, a man who knew that position meant everything*

Becoming the Author of Your Brand

Once you have defined your target brand persona, you can start to create a plan to move forward, evolve, and begin to show up in the way that will attract the people, relationships, and opportunities you want in your life. Ultimately, this is about challenging yourself to grow and gain confidence and competence, which you can do through careful review and goal setting in the following areas.

Character: who you are, what you value. Do you live what you say you believe in? Do you honor commitments? Do you need to monitor your actions and reactions more closely? Do you need to manage resources, time, and money more wisely?

Reputation: what others say about you when you are not around. Can people count on you? Do they say things about you that they don't feel they could say to you? Do you keep your word? Do you reflect the best service to others?

Expertise: what you know and authority you hold. Is your knowledge deep enough, wide enough, current enough? Do you need more education, on-the-job mentoring, industry networking? Are you stretching yourself up to the next level?

Vision: what you are passionate about, what you want to achieve. Are your dreams big enough, bold enough, and audacious enough? Do you have the confidence to strike down limiting beliefs and embrace the concept that you have the potential to achieve more than your parents, your colleagues, and your network?

Career History: what you have done, the professional experiences you hold. Does your resume reflect your potential, consistency, and accomplishments? Do you need to set intentions to move further faster?

Personal Style: how you present yourself in person. Does how you care for yourself properly reflect how you care

35

for other things? Are you always putting your best foot forward? Does your presence demonstrate competence, success, or wealth? Are you clean, crisp, and contemporary?

Visibility: how others find you or see you in person or online. How often do you leave the four walls of your office to network? Where can you be found on social sites? How many conversations do you have a week to keep contacts active? Are you living your brand attributes when others connect with you, or is the old you still showing up?

- Website
- Social media profile
- Google search results

Network: whom you know and who knows you. Are you actively introducing yourself to new contacts? Do you belong to associations, volunteer, or take courses? Are you focused on expanding yourself and your network? Are you seeking out people from whom you can learn and who can help you envision the next move up?

To ensure that your brand is perceived how you would like it to be perceived, it needs to be reflected in all these areas consistently with your desired brand attributes driving goals, connections, conversations, focus, and intention. For example, you cannot seek to be known as a dynamic, friendly, successful leader if your appearance is always scruffy or unkempt, if you make promises that you don't keep, or if you are constantly getting into political arguments or over-posting pictures of your dressed-up dog on Facebook.

The details of your personal brand will directly correlate to the level of influence you will attain and the type of connections you will make. Remember, you can only claim to be a 'mover and shaker' if your network contains other movers and shakers. Develop the right brand, and you will do more to attract the right people and opportunities.

My advice: set out to create a magnificent personal brand, and then challenge yourself to step into it each and every day.

Life doesn't give you what you want, it gives you what you are. —*Nido R Qubein, master motivational speaker, leader, and influencer raising up the next generation of thinkers and leaders at High Point University*

Takeaways

☐ Your brand is what people say about you when you're not in the room.

☐ Your brand needs to inspire trust. If you achieve that, your fans will build your network in your absence.

☐ You need to take ownership of your brand, make it intentional, and give people an impression that reflects what you wish to be known for, and it needs to be designed for where you want to be, not where you currently are.

5

Measure Your Connective Health

You must fully understand and embrace that you and only you are in control of your own personal economy.

Your goal on this journey is to protect your economic situation as best you can from the violent swings of industry, stock markets, governments, and natural events. Think about how we judge the economic indicators of a country or the credit score of the individual. Why then would we not measure our Connective Health Score? How wide is your world of connections? Do you have the right connections at the right level, in the right industries, and with the right access to other people's cash? Will your connections be able to help carry you through difficult economic times?

No longer can any of us afford to go for the simple when it comes to work. 'Simple' will deliver neither survival nor success.

You must learn to think about your career and business on multiple levels. You can never have only one thing going for you—one paycheck, career path, or ambition—because if that one thing is taken away, you will have nothing. You must always be in growth and expansion mode, gaining knowledge and developing new avenues of income. And key to all of this is you must be constantly expanding personal connections because these connections will bring you both business intelligence and opportunity.

One of my business coaches has a phrase that he tells all his clients, "It's not only whom you know; it's who knows you." I loved this philosophy from the first moment I heard it, but today I would adjust the phrase thus:

It's not only whom you know; it's who will find you in their time of need.

Your value to the world of business is directly related to how well you are connected and how you can solve problems and deliver results. If you are not where you need to be today, if you do not know enough of the right people, then you need to get started. Think of it this way—you need to build your ark before it rains.

Don't care what others say; don't let their opinions hold you back. Think big, think mighty, think life-saving. Set your sights on establishing a mega-network.

Building an expansive network takes time and intention. We need to plant the seeds, then water and nurture them. And once they are underway, plant the next row of seeds.

And to be clear, we are not only looking to get names on our lists and in our phones. We're looking to build relationships, build trust, and ultimately, build business. All of this takes time, planning, and effort.

How powerful are the key individuals in your network today? Let's do a little test. If you were to find yourself out of work right now, how many people could you contact today who could either offer you an opportunity or refer you to someone who might be able to offer you a position?

If you're an entrepreneur, the question is similar. If you needed to make a sale today, how many people could you contact right now to recommend you or your products and services to someone else?

Take five minutes and write the names of your best contacts in the box below:

How did you do?

- Twenty-five names or more is excellent.

- Ten names or more is good.
- Five names or more is a start.
- If you have fewer than three names on your list, you need to do a lot of work.

For each name on the list, you are going to determine a score based on the last time you were in contact with that person. Was it last week, last month, six months ago, last year, or even longer? For any connection with which you have had contact within the last three months, write a number three beside that name; if it was in the last six months, write a two; the last year, write a one; and if it has been over a year, sorry, you get a zero.

- If you have 25 or more points, you're doing very well.
- If you have 15 or more points, that's too not bad.
- But if you have less than 10 points, the chances are that you will not be able to use your network to help you generate business or find a new job quickly.

How Wide and Deep Is Your Network Today?

The strength of your connective health is also determined by how many **unique business connections** you have. Let's review ways in which you can assess your Connective Health Score related to your unique connections. Read the following and think about your answers to these questions.

1. Are you set up on LinkedIn? If so,
   - How many connections do you have?
   - How many recommendations or testimonials do you have?
   - How many countries are you connected to?
   - How many companies are you connected to?
   - How many groups are you in?

- How many senior managers and CEOs are you connected to?
- How are you using these social sites to connect with and show people your expertise?

2. Are you connected on other social platforms: Facebook, Twitter, Instagram, WhatsApp, and more?
   - How many connections do you have?
   - How many countries are you connected to?
   - How many companies are you connected to?
   - How many groups are you in?
   - How many senior managers and CEOs are you connected to?
   - How often do you give testimonials or endorsements, like a post, or interact in another way?

3. Do you keep contacts on your phone? How many contacts do you have? For how many are you sure the information is up to date?

4. How many email addresses are in your address book? How many of these are up to date? Are you connected to all these people on LinkedIn?

5. If you're an entrepreneur or run a small business, how many contacts do you have on your mailing list? Do you have a consistent practice for growing your list? How frequently do you contact your list, providing relevant information, good news, or special offers? And just how much do you know about your clients, subscribers, and fans?

6. What associations do you belong to? How many other members also belong? Have you set up your online

profile? Do you get engaged in special interest groups or face-to-face events? Are you connecting to these contacts on LinkedIn?

Although the quality of powerful network connections is important, we must build a reasonably sized network too. You cannot afford to risk your future by limiting your possibilities or investing in a few connections. Embrace the vision of a network—deep and wide, far and near, young and old.

While there is no ideal answer to the question, "How many connections should you have?" being able to measure where you stand today and establishing targets for where you would like to be will improve your Connective Health Score.

Establish a Goal to Measure and Improve Your Connective Health Score

Let's use LinkedIn as a benchmark. With over 470 million user profiles growing at around 17 million per quarter, LinkedIn is the biggest business connecting platform. (Unless you are speaking Mandarin; then you may focus elsewhere.)

Based on the statistics below, you should target having at least one thousand unique connections to have a solid Connective Health Score. This will put you in the top 30 percent of active users and greatly enhance your opportunities to be seen and heard.

# of Connections	% of LinkedIn Users
0 - 499	43%
500 - 999	27%
1000 - 2999	17%
3000+	13%

And if you want to take a leap to join the ranks of the super connectors, you need to be looking at creating a network of three thousand unique connections. But also remember, LinkedIn is for so much more than just keeping track of people. You can share updates, post blogs, and engage with your community once you focus on using this program to its fullest capacity.

There are some other tools you can use to calculate your online influence, such as Klout. Klout takes into account not only the number of followers and connections you have across most social media platforms but also your level of activity and the level of engagement by others. While this is an interesting tool, it is more a measure of your social media influence than your business influence. However, if you are curious, log on and link your social accounts. The average Klout Score is 40, but if you get 50 or above, you are doing great with influence and engagement on social media platforms. To be in the top 5 percent of all users, you need to get your score to 63.

> **A note about social sites**. Unless you have unlimited time—and none of us do—you cannot be in all places at once, so select wisely where you wish to be. There are great tools to help you manage your posts, but even with the rights tools and resources, do not feel pressured to be everywhere. Your business and networking opportunities should be the first priority; selecting social sites should be at best your second.

Take a moment to complete the self-explanatory table on the next page to give yourself a quick assessment of your current connective footprint.

Connect to Influence

Connection Source	Today	6 months	12 months
Business			
Mobile Phone Contact List			
Electronic Address Book			
LinkedIn			
Skype/Facetime			
Other			
Total			
Social			
Facebook			
Twitter			
Instagram			
Pinterest			
Other			
Total			
Network			
Courses/prof development			
Association			
Club			
Sport			
Worship			
Other			
Total			
Total connections benchmark			

Thinking about growing your connections can be intimidating whether you are just starting or trying to elevate your impact, but it can be easy once you set a goal and focus.

One year my New Year's resolution was specifically to increase my number of LinkedIn contacts. This was when I wanted to have over five hundred connections so when people looked at my profile it no longer had a specific number but it flipped to 500+. I wanted to give the impression I was someone worth knowing, so nearly every day for two months I invested about ten minutes a day looking for people to link to (coworkers from my past, school friends, industry contacts, etc.) and groups to join. (Did you know you can join many groups but make them invisible to people who view you? So go ahead and join). It didn't take long, and I achieved that first target.

Another year, my goal was to join a new professional association so that I could expand my business contacts and bring more information back to my job. While there are many membership organizations to choose from, I joined the American Marketing Association. With the AMA not only did I get engaged, grow my relationships, and gain knowledge, I was also able to work my way up to serve as my chapter's president. This greatly improved the quality of my connections and helped open doors for me.

Little did I know that one day on a business trip in China I would be interviewed by media who had tagged me as an American marketing expert all because they reviewed my LinkedIn profile and saw this.

Honestly, as you work through this book and plan to be a super connector, you have to believe that you never know where the opportunities will be waiting for you if you just keep yourself open. Are you ready to move forward and intentionally grow your community of supporters so they can find you in their time of need?

You build sway by taking small but consistent action, offline and online, to convey your character, your competence, and your charisma. —Sima Dahl, *America's Personal Branding Champion*^{TM}*, super connector, woman of influence, believer that a great wine makes for great networking*

Takeaways

☐ Building your network takes planning, time, and effort, and you need to do it before you need it.

☐ Assessing the strength and depth of your current network will help you establish a vision and goals for where you want to be.

☐ We need to be building a LinkedIn network with at least 1,000 connections to be in the top 17 percent or over 3,000 if we want to get into the top 13 percent.

References:

Linkedin connection statistics.
https://www.statista.com/statistics/264097/number-of-1st-level-connections-of-linkedin-users/

Linkedin user number statistics.
https://www.statista.com/statistics/274050/quarterly-numbers-of-linkedin-members/

6

Cultivate Your Community

Three challenges:

Imagine that someone asks you to solve a problem. The neurons in your brain begin sparking, and thoughts and images come together based on your personal experiences and knowledge. But your experiences—as good as they may seem to you—are limited. Now, envision a circle over your head, and fill that circle with dots representing your information and experiences. To solve the problem, you began drawing lines from dot to dot to develop ideas. But what if your dots could reach out of your circle and connect to the dots hanging over the head of someone else? With this capability, you could multiply the available ideas and outcomes in immeasurable ways. In this way, your network serves as a **force multiplier**.

Imagine that someone asks you to see around a corner. This represents a simple request, but from where you stand you haven't been given the gift of x-ray vision. Therefore, you cannot see through the solid wall.

But what if you could ask a friend to hold up a mirror that would let you see around the corner—like those on the ramp in a parking garage? What if that mirror could reflect to you what is around that corner? You didn't move at all, yet you have been transported so that you can see what was previously blocked by a wall. Through connections with others you can develop **periscope vision**.

Imagine that someone asks you to retrieve a flag from the top of a mountain. You can proudly make each step and transverse the rocky terrain, sweating and huffing as you make your ascent, or you can simply find the gondola operator and swiftly make your way up to the top. Using other people's acquired skills can get you where you want to go faster than you can do it alone. Linking to experts will enable you to have a **shortcut to resources**. As you chart your course for success, the first thing you need to realize is that you do not need to go it alone. In fact, the best way to achieve success is through leveraging connective intelligence.

If you want to go quickly, go alone. If you want to go far, go together. —African proverb and statement that just makes sense

For most people, this is not new information. In fact, getting ahead through whom you know is one of the oldest tricks in the book, but what is surprising is that rarely, if ever, do people set about with a true strategic intent to build their personal networks. And that is the decision and commitment I am asking you to make as you continue to work through this book. You must believe that more than anything your priority in business today has to be to build a world-class network of personal consultants, coaches, connectors, and confidants who can help elevate you to the next level of your life.

So, I ask you, if you are the sum of the people closest to you, what is your net potential value today?

If you don't design your life plan, chances are you'll fall into someone else's plan. And guess what they have planned for you? Not much. —*Jim Rohn, leader in the direct sales industry, expert at knocking on doors and overcoming rejection on his path to greatness*

Connective Vision

Success can come to you if you are intent on:

1. Establishing a personal vision and
2. Charting your course to collect and cultivate your community of supporters.

As with any solid business plan, you must have goals, objectives, and a system for measurement. Jot down some answers to the following questions:

- What industry is your expertise in?
- Where do you stand today in your career?
- Are you happy with your job level or title?
- What is your annual income?
- What is your personal net worth (assets compared to liabilities)?
- What are you known for?
- Who knows you?

Now consider the next set of questions:

- What do you want to be different in twelve months?
- What do you want to change about work?
- What do you want your annual income to be?
- How many income streams do you want to have?
- How do you want your personal net worth to change?
- What do you wish to be known for?
- If you lost your job tomorrow, who would help you get a new one?

♦ If you started a business tomorrow, who would be your first customer?

In today's business environment, your net worth is your network. It is that simple. You must be connected.

Most people see education as the answer to achieving life's success, but that is not always the case. At one point in my career I was at a crossroads, and I went into my boss and announced that I was going to begin a master's program. From behind his desk, he looked at me and calmly responded, "It is your choice what you do with your life, but if you want to succeed here, you have to learn this business."

He went on and explained how business was not in the office or a classroom, but business was out in the field where the customers were and where other industry people were. He said that one learns by meeting and doing. At that moment, I traded academics for airplanes and made my advancements through experiences and connections with people.

The higher education path is noble, but it is not the only way. If you want 'suite' success with a position in the C-suite, then you must increase your ability to establish a grand vision, commit to action, and connect with the right people who will help you along. Think of it this way; you just can't achieve the highest levels of success within the confinement of the four walls where you currently sit. You need to hold a vision and expectation for more in life.

As you work to establish your vision and undertake the steps to make it a reality, this book will request that you challenge your thinking and write responses so your subconscious mind and your conscious mind can work in the same direction. Once I was explaining to a friend my frustration at being in a phase of life where I couldn't get ahead. I explained how badly I wanted to get to the next level and didn't seem able to reach it.

Her response to me was simple, "You are sending mixed signals to the universe." She recognized that I had verbalized my intent and created actions; however, she noted that I could also be filled with self-doubt and spread my focus across other areas not critical to my desired path. She explained that the universe prefers order and not chaos, and I needed to gain clarity of vision and figure out how to reduce the drama and doubt in my life. So this is the hard lesson I learned that maybe you can learn quicker than I did:

If your intention and focus are clear, the universe will deliver to you what you set your mind on. If your intention and focus is unclear, the universe will deliver you a chaotic path forward.

The point I am trying to share is that you can move forward in an aimless way accepting any connections that land in your lap, or you can choose to connect and navigate your way to opportunities and success with intention and purpose. I suggest the latter if it is your goal to get ahead in life faster.

Work diligently to craft your vision. Take time for quiet and reflective thought. Consider what groups of people you need to increase your interactions with. How will you get the attention of the right people at work or in your industry? What might you need to develop and change in yourself to make leaps forward?

It is not an easy task to see into your future, but if you can construct your future in your mind's eye, it will evolve. You are playing the long game in life, and you should have big goals. Being clear on expectations and goals will help you navigate your choices, your investment of time, and the connections that you choose to make.

Be confident that what your mind focuses on it will find a way to achieve. When you create tension in your mind and then set your sights on something you want, your mind will seek opportunities to resolve the tension. It is as if you are taking a Slinky toy and stretching it forward—the result is that the back of the Slinky desperately wants to move forward to relieve the strain on the coils.

I challenge you to stretch your vision as far as you can, and imagine the people it will cause you to meet on your journey forward.

Connective Value

Think about the people in your network today and then think about the people you wish were in your network. Like any business venture, you are only as good as your partners, vendors, and customers, so you must outline goals for the types of people you want in your personal network. And these goals should be huge.

If you want to be more, achieve more, and influence more, you need to seek out people of high connective value, people who are significantly ahead of you in success, knowledge, and personal net worth. Your hands must be reaching upward. You must acknowledge and even celebrate that each handshake and smile will take you closer to the things you desire—even if you don't know how.

Viewing people in terms of their connective value is the difference between thinking exponentially versus linearly— the possibilities held in each handshake are infinite. —Me,

Cultivate Your Community

Allison Summers, global influence and empowerment authority, mother, chocolate lover, world traveler, protector of keeping people relevant to the business world

When you are operating in the mode of connective value, you think vast and wide. You must be intent on connecting with people bigger than you and people who stand wider and deeper than you in their networks.

You must think about your personal connections both vertically and horizontally, linking to people working in the same industry as well as to individuals in the same line of professional practice. For example, if you are in the medical field, your vertical channel would be others in the medical field, but your horizontal channel would be people across other professional segments such as finance, accounting, sales, marketing, technology, and operations. You will find that once you grow the right connections, your network will have its own pulse and will sustain your business life.

What can new connections do for you? People of high connective value help you fulfill these needs and objectives:
- Increase channels to new connections
- Elevate opportunities
- Serve as a professional role model or coach
- Provide a brain trust to solve problems
- Lend viewpoints from a skill set you do not have (financial, technology, marketing, etc.)
- Serve as a mirror for a future you can't yet see
- Connect you to insights from the top
- Raise your brand cache just by being in the same circle
- Teach you the language of business executives
- Show you what life is like as a 'top-percent' income earner

Take some time to write a wish list of people whom you would like to meet. This may actually be a very hard task, so do not be afraid to document a description of the people if you do not know actual names. Some examples of what may be on your list could be the title of the head of a company, a person in the same position as you but at a competitive company, an author or famous speaker, a community leader, a politician, or an editor of an industry magazine. You may describe types of people you want to connect to, such as industry leaders, top marketers, professional recruiters.

Do not limit the list of possibilities because of perceived inaccessibility—limiting the list at this point is putting limitations on the potential of your tomorrow.

Your Big, Bold, and Brash Connection Wish List

On the chart below, write names or types of people you wish to connect with. Make this list as wild and crazy as you need to set the bar high; let your subconscious guide you.

When you finish this book, come back to look at your list. At that point, maybe you'll want to add more or change them, but you need to be aware that you have to establish goals for the types of people you want to meet.

My Big, Bold Top 5	
People	Industry/Expertise
1	
2	
3	
4	
5	

INFLUENCE

Connective Course

One point of the above exercise is to take a hard look at whom you know today and whom you need to know. Let me correct that—not 'need' but whom you 'must' know. It will be very clear when you survey the list you have made that there is a gap between where you stand now and how to know these people who are so far ahead of you, and only by filling that gap will you be able to work at a fast pace toward your future. I fully recognize that finding these connections will not be a simple task, but nonetheless you must work on your strategic intent for growing your community.

You need to construct a real plan for seeking out and spending time with the leaders in your industry and the other spaces you have identified. Plotting your course will take thought, time, and money, but you can't think about the cost of the pursuit. Rather, you must think about the return on the investment you will receive in the future. People who have money know they can only spend each dollar once, but the difference is that they will spend the dollar if they know it will return more dollars to them in the future.

If you are worried about time, it is clear you love your couch more than success. In truth, most of us, even as working parents or those juggling a job and continuing studies, can and do find some time each week to dedicate to cultivating our path to the future.

Armed with your connective vision, you should consider all the places and ways you can grow your community. Some ways to make contacts may include:
- Bolster your social media profile and presence
- Renew and refresh past connections
- Ask a business leader you know about his/her secret to building a great network

- Ask someone to an informational lunch where you can learn more about what he/she does and ask if he/she can introduce you to anyone in his/her network
- Hire a business coach
- Link into a mastermind group
- Tap into alumni networks
- Join a professional trade association
- Join a chamber of commerce
- Attend an international convention or local professional development training (even if you must pay)
- Volunteer in a service club organization (Rotary, Kiwanis, Lions, Zonta, Moose, etc.)
- Give back in a charity setting; attend black-tie galas and fundraising events
- Join Toastmasters (and improve public speaking skills at the same time)
- Take a university course
- Get an industry certification
- Offer to speak for industry webinars
- Submit an article to an industry magazine
- Seek out seminars on wealth management
- Start a blog or a podcast or post articles on Medium or other platforms
- Go to a 'wild card' event—a free speaker at a hotel, a pitch to go into direct sales, an event at the library

Items on the above list may sound meaningless and time consuming, but if you don't select a starting point for working toward your goal, you will be standing in the same place next year as you are today. Make up your mind that you will select some vehicle or method to make (at minimum) three new high-value connections a month. If the activity you select doesn't yield the results you are looking for, then move to another option.

You must think of yourself as building a 'world class' community, and if you are meeting people but not the right people, you must move on. This is the business of you, and you need to collect smart and brilliant people who will guide you to your future.

Go big and wide. I will say it again: **Go big and wide!** Ensure that you are setting a purposeful course to open your trade routes to economic opportunities.

Measure Your Progress

Your connective health score is important, and as you move along your journey, you should have a constant awareness of your progress. There is a business saying, "What gets measured, gets mastered."

In the last chapter, you marked a baseline for where you stand. Now, you must consider measuring your personal key performance indicators (KPI's) for success. Will it be:

+ By the type and number of new connections in social media?
+ By the amount of one-on-one meetings you have?
+ By the number of people accepting your phone calls?
+ By the size of the audience subscribing to your blog?
+ Directly related to increased income such as new customers, closed deals, and sales figures?

Congratulations for being focused and setting your course. Once you commit to forward movement, you will see your trade routes begin to open before you.

Takeaways

☐ Create a plan for the future you desire. Include the revenue streams, the desired income, the industries you want to work in, and the positions that you want to hold.

☐ Establish your connective vision, and identify those people or types of people whom you need to add to your network in order to achieve your goals. Don't forget to add those people who know the people you need to know, and leverage those connections. Go big and wide.

☐ Create a plan to start to build a network of the high-value connections that you need to achieve your career and life goals, and track and monitor your progress. Know what gets measured gets mastered.

7

Invest in the Right Opportunities

Your decision to make connecting a best practice in your life is admirable. Obviously, you have made it a priority, or you would not have read this far. Even if you must pass through uncertainty and discomfort, you ultimately know that connection into other people's intelligence, experiences, resources, cash, and capital offers the best pathway to attaining your future economic sustainability and wealth.

As with any activity you invest time in, they do not all hold equal value on the return for time and energy invested. I really like chocolate bars, they make me feel wonderful when I hang out with them, and honestly, they love me back throughout each and every bite. But my friend the chocolate bar does little to help my physical being sustain itself, so for that I must consciously take in a diet packed with a far greater nutritional value.

You can think of your connective encounters this way as well. Some people will be sweet to be around, but realistically, they will do little or nothing for your business and work life. It is easy to be drawn to that which you enjoy, but you have to remain focused on what you need that will help build your influence.

It's great to spend time at a networking event with someone you know and like. But that's not what you're there for.

Your goal is to expand your network by meeting new people.
—*Beth Ramsey, a shining lady who founded the Brilliance Network*^{TM}
so that others could shine as well

We all have the same amount of time. The humbling reality for everyone is that once we use time, we never get it back. Thus, you must be in the business of time well spent.

The difference between highly successful individuals and the individuals in the back of the ranks is how we expend time, energy, and focus. While connecting is vital, I understand more than anyone that it is not the only practice that will set you up for great achievements in life. However, without the ability to develop relationships, your ability to take your personal wealth to the highest level will also be limited. This means you must learn how to become an efficient connector, developing working rules for how and to whom you extend your connective energy and precious time.

The Importance of Competent Relationship Building Applies to Everyone

Recently, I read an article in which the author implied that the great entrepreneurs and business leaders of the modern world—like Edison, Disney, Zuckerberg, and Jobs—were likely so brilliant they didn't need to worry about networking and relationships. However, I would argue that brilliance only carries you so far. At the end of the day, you must get other people to buy into you, your value, and your grand vision if you are going to reach your goals. If you cannot connect with others on your own terms, you have to either rely on others for relationship-building assistance or forge ahead over a bumpy road to success. Ask any entrepreneur seeking to gain a major financial investment from a venture capitalist, and he will tell you no matter how great the idea or the presentation, people are still investing in people.

The Importance of Effectively and Efficiently Gathering Connective Intelligence Applies to Everyone

Everyone you will meet can have worth to you. Everyone. The applied wisdom for connecting will be in how you view each encounter and how much energy you will dedicate to it. For me, there are three levels of priority I assign in my mind when talking with people or reading their social channels. So I ask this question, "Are they valuable to me in the moment, in the maybe, or in the must?"

At a glance, the three levels can be explained like this:
In the Moment—Jump in, get information, and get out.
In the Maybe—Exert modest effort, gain some knowledge, and capture the contact for future reference.
In the Must—Recognize the great potential for significant knowledge transfer and business opportunities, and therefore do whatever you can to capture the contact and follow up.

In the Moment

Once you embrace a policy of connecting, you will find there are real possibilities to have meaningful conversations with new people everywhere you look. The goals you will have for people whom you place in the 'In the Moment' category will be very different than the other levels, but nonetheless, do not miss the opportunity to connect, secure what you can, and move along.

Wherever I go and whatever I do, my small talk with others always leads to business topics, world travel, and cultural differences. I have a natural curiosity to learn more about business models and how people make profits, as well as how societal views and economies compare, contrast, and are faring in other countries.

Sometimes when you do choose to speak with people whom you may think are inconsequential, you can learn the most amazing things. For example, have you ever asked a cab driver how his business is going? They can usually tell you very quickly the math on what it costs to cover their license, operator medallions, insurance, gas, repairs, maintenance, and so on in order to tell you how much they must average hourly in fares to clear a profit for the day. And most cab drivers in the US do more than just drive cabs. I have met drivers working on a PhD thesis, playing dad to five kids by day and driving by night, and selling insurance out of the front seat between fares. Which simply reminds me, just because I see people as they are in a specific moment, that moment does not contain all their hopes and dreams.

And I have gained all sorts of odd knowledge by taking time and focusing intently on conversations with my chance encounters. I know a little about the challenges of retaining skilled workers in third-world countries, how oil rigs work in the Gulf of Mexico, what the job requirements are for a train conductor, and that in recent years Dubai has served as home to the most cranes in the world due to booming construction. I have met Frenchmen heading home from a month playing cowboy on a Montana ranch and spoken to African safari rangers who have big dreams of seeing black bears and grizzly bears in Yellowstone National Park. If you take time to talk to people, you can learn amazing things. Some of these things you can take back and apply in business; other information will merely round out your ability to hold a meaningful conversation in other encounters.

I firmly believe there is a direct correlation between the more knowledge you gather and your ability to formulate wisdom for your life and for your world views. I know businesspeople who will proudly profess that they read ten newspapers and magazines a day. That will give them data and facts, but through people you gain so much more. You gain experiences and can embrace them as your own.

In the end, treat the people you meet in the moment with as much respect and acceptance as if that moment was all that mattered. Meet on common ground somehow, in some way; just be brave and speak, even if all the time allows is to offer a compliment, ask a name, or discover where they are from, what brought them here, how they like it. What makes playing 'In the Moment' so wonderful is that you can practice appreciating people, and there is no right or wrong result. Practice appreciating people, and it will positively come back to you.

In the Maybe

Most people you meet through business meetings, networking events, and social exchanges will fall under the 'In the Maybe' category. Likely you already have something in common with this group just through the way you meet. You will employ the skills and knowledge you have gained through becoming an exceptional connector, but in general, you will exert low effort and capture contact details.

Your conversations and exchanges should progress as if you are a detective seeking to uncover if this person offers anything that you could use in the future. You are also seeing if there is anything valuable you can provide to him.

The people in the maybe group are important because someday there just may be a pearl in the oyster. Perhaps today you have nothing to offer each other, but tomorrow you may find that you are better off reconnecting and working together. So for this initial meeting, you simply maintain a cheerful and engaging disposition and evaluate the return on investment for the energy you place into remaining in contact.

However, this may also be the group that puts up the most barriers to connecting. You may find that people beneath you and people above you may be easier to connect with than those in the range close to you. There are a few reasons for this. The first is that they may not have developed the right skills yet, and they just don't know how to reciprocate connecting. It may be that they are sizing you up and don't see enough value in the promise of how you present yourself to be motivated to connect. They may see you as a threat and then are not inclined to offer you a hand up. It might have nothing to do with you; they could simply be preoccupied with something else and don't know how to keep personal issues out of business. Or they may be afraid that you are just out to sell to them and therefore won't give up their personal data. Regardless of the reason, know that there will be people who want nothing to do with you, and that's okay. Save your energy for those people who are receptive and want to play the game. Frankly, the closed individuals are not likely going anywhere very rapidly in life.

In the Must

I enjoy all my networking adventures, but I get downright giddy when I make what I believe is an extraordinary connection. Yes, I said giddy. Not a great visual picture and not a professional term by any means, but I don't know how else to explain it. Sometimes you meet people whom you find smart, intelligent, and defiant compared to the norm. These are business leaders who can offer you expert help or market insights or potential customers who may lead to a financial boost in your business.

At times, you meet people whose company you deeply enjoy. Even if you can't explain why, you know you must meet them again. Then there are subject experts to whom you will connect and follow blogs or twitter feeds because through them you can fill a knowledge gap. In other instances, you meet talented achievers who have accomplished something extraordinary, and merely being in their presence or having them in your network makes you feel better and brighter. Whatever the reason, when you get that stirring feeling in your soul, you know you simply have to make the connection.

Pulling a good network together takes effort, sincerity, and time. —*Alan Collins, founder Success in HR, longtime professional observer of the traits and talents that take people to the top, unapologetic Chicago Bulls fan*

When you put people in the 'must' category, seek the extraordinary over the ordinary. You should recognize that this group needs a proper balance of extra attention yet managed restraint. If this group is truly comprised of exceptional people, they likely have limited time and would appreciate your contact but also your brevity. You must convey to this group that you know how to speak in executive terms, and you need to be sure you have developed business acumen.

Someday You Will Be the Magnet

The remarkable thing about network building is that with steady and consistent activity, people will begin to refer others to you without much effort on your part. People will also find you on their own because you have worked to build a strong relationship network and digital footprint. It is an amazing feeling when that happens. Think again about what

I said early in this book, **It's not only whom you know, but it's who will find you in their time of need.**

As you start your journey, your goal will be to consider everyone you meet as a potential contact and to sort them into three categories: in the moment, in the maybe, and in the must. But as you move forward, you will naturally become more selective in whom you wish to connect to and where you place your relationship energy. As you take leaps forward you will see that an individual whom you once put in the 'must' category will necessarily be pushed down into the 'maybe' category. When that happens, it means you have progressed appropriately.

Never underestimate how much the people at the top will notice your connections and your professional presence. Because these people have limited time, they will determine whether to allow you into their contact circle based on what you have done, whom you know, and if someone they know knows and trusts you. This is the level you want to get to, for this is where influence is at play and money is made.

Even when you become the magnet, do not lose the drive to be building your connections. You will always need to be on the lookout to identify supporting talent, to spot new trends, and to find new markets.

Your connections will serve as the gateway to opportunity. Cherish them, nurture them, and when you can, take them along your trade route with you.

Takeaways

☐ Treat everyone you meet with respect, but don't waste too much time with people who add little to your network just because they are nice. Your focus has to be on building the right connections, not just any connections.

☐ Learn to analyze quickly your new connections to determine whether they are in the moment, in the maybe, or in the must, and act accordingly.

☐ As you build your network, you will become a magnet where people will start to seek you out.

8

Value People

We are all unique human beings differentiated by personality, experience, culture, mood, perception, prejudices, language, customs, mind-set, stress, fear, legalities, cautions, gender, motivation, knowledge, objectives, and responsibilities. When you encounter someone for the first time you have no idea where he or she is in the journey of the day or where life has taken that one before that moment.

When you smile or reach out your hand or give a slight bow, you do it as a gesture of faith—faith that somehow you will find some point of commonality with the person who stands before you even if, in fact, you have very little in common. A connection is therefore a promise that you will accept, respect, and have a positive exchange with the person before you. However, the dimension of human interaction is so diverse that not all initial connections go well.

If you don't like something, change it. If you can't change it, change your attitude. —Maya Angelou, *promoter of self-examination, equality, and friendship; civil rights activist, author, and slamming poet*

In the first installment of my professional life, pre-business, I was an educator. When I was at university, I had a professor who one day uttered the wisest statement I had heard during my entire academic career, and that wisdom I have carried with me to this day. This professor was a young female, who wore business suits and always had her hair pulled up in a tight bun. It was her mission to ensure that we knew how to relate to six-year-olds and prepare them for the daunting challenges of first grade.

In one session, she was trying to explain the realities of teaching in rural Oklahoma. She described what school life was like in an impoverished community that was scarce on jobs, prospects, and even the most fundamental resources. She explained how students came to school unwashed, unfed, and unruly. She told of students who smelled so bad that they had to be washed and fed before the school day could begin.

We sat in that room and listened to her, wide-eyed, with our minds conjuring up images to match her story. She explained to us that her job was simply to move the students forward no matter the circumstance and no matter in what state she received them. She said, "You don't have to like someone to love him forward." This was a profound thought for me. "You don't have to like someone to love him. . . ."

My teacher wasn't telling us about hugging and holding the students. It wasn't that kind of love. She was talking about loving them enough to invest in them today and shape them for their tomorrow. It was about accepting where they were and helping move them forward to where they needed to be. That was the way she saw love. She didn't condemn based on the current state but could envision a future state she could usher these tiny human beings into.

Certainly, if each of us could apply this philosophy to life's encounters, perhaps we could have different outcomes. If we understood that our job was not to 'like' all the people we met but to 'love' them by accepting them for where they are at that point in time, if we understood that having a positive or meaningful exchange with someone had nothing to do with if we liked him/her or if he/she liked us but was more about what needed to be done, would we spend much of our emotional energy in a different way?

How many people have you had to work with in life whom you didn't like? How much time did you spend focusing on what that person did that bothered you, trying to figure out what he was thinking, or telling others how much you didn't like him rather than just working things through? Overthinking things—a.k.a. creating your own drama—making everything personal, or being nit-picky and critical fosters a destructive mind-set that will never serve you well.

But what if you can look at people and situations differently? What if your role in human interactions is to think about how you can offer 'love' to move someone or something forward? When it comes to getting things done, your eye is on the long game and not on the roadblocks that others may be placing before you.

Nobody cares how much you know, until they know how much you care. —*Theodore Roosevelt, twenty-sixth President of the United States, reformer and environmentalist before it was cool*

When you operate this way, people will notice the difference. Think about the fact that even in the smallest interactions, people can read you. In order to reach the level of being a super connector, you must rise above immediate thoughts of negativity. Stop judging, start listening, and move forward in each moment.

Ultimately, at the heart of love is acceptance. And all people want to be accepted no matter their background or position in life. You must figure out how to project authentic acceptance of the people whom you will meet in life.

As a business leader, I have had employees, coworkers, and clients who, if I allowed them to, could absolutely drive me crazy. But if you can learn to rise above the 'small-mindedness' of only working with people you personally like, you can achieve great things. If you can remind yourself that you do not need to like someone to show him or her acceptance, opportunities will open up for you.

The next time you are interacting with someone and it feels awkward or tense, remind yourself: *This is a situation where I have permission to recognize that I may not like the person before me, but I can certainly appreciate that this interaction is still valuable. I know there is a job to be done, and I can find a way forward. I can respect the end goal enough that I can treat the person before me with courtesy and acceptance.*

When challenged, think of the way a teacher loves a student. The student may be full of faults, he may not do what he is supposed to do, and he may not always use respectful behaviors, but it is the teacher's job to nurture him forward, to engage different tactics to achieve the learning, to move the individual from the desk of a first grader to the desk of a twelfth grader.

People don't always know what they are doing or how their behaviors are coming across. Sometimes they don't know because no one was brave enough to tell them. Can you love someone enough to guide her gently? Can you love someone enough to connect with him where he is and still move business forward?

"You don't have to like someone to love him" stands as the best advice I was ever given in my life, and I hope you can grow to see the wisdom in it as well. Whatever else you can offer them, how you make others feel will determine the strength of the connection you develop.

Spread love everywhere you go. Let no one ever come to you without leaving happier. —Mother Teresa, small-town girl from Skopje who managed to make a difference in the world to those whom no one liked

Takeaways

- [ ] Not all the initial connections are going to go well, but with a bit of persistence and effort you can turn them around.
- [ ] You don't have to like someone to create a positive encounter or connection with him or her.
- [ ] When you show people that you care about them, it will help you create a very strong connection.

9

Turn up Your CHARMS

A great connector is prepared for what happens beyond the 'pitch.' Yes, the practice of delivering a concise and compelling pitch (stating the business you are in, the results you generate, and the value that you offer) is critical to generate interest and convey your value. However, it must then be backed up with the impression that not only will you deliver, but you are a person others want to be around and want to do business with.

Super connectors know that their behaviors must convey a joyful and easy experience. And these behaviors are really simple enough for anyone to add to his/her skill set. To be likeable, you must know how to turn on your CHARMS.

Create comfort
Hear with your eyes
Avoid too much self
Relate relevantly
Match styles
Share something of value

Create Comfort

People are drawn to the comfort of warm and inviting spaces. Comfort means ease, joy, acceptance, and warmth all rolled into a moment. But how can comfort best be conveyed in a thirty-second exchange? Here are some tips to incorporate into your connection practices.

Image that there is a three-foot circle around your body and this imaginary space represents your home. Imagine that anyone who steps into this space has entered your home, and it is your goal to make a positive impact with your hospitality. Consider how you behave when you open your front door and find your best friend standing on the porch. Of course, you excitedly greet him/her and usher him/her in.

Now imagine the feeling that you want that individual to experience. Are you running all over the place, picking things up, and being hurried in the kitchen? Or are you grounded in the moment? Imagine that through the heels of your feet you can feel a direct connection to the floor, that you are standing steadfast and sturdy, that your shoulders are back and chest lifted, demonstrating that you are open for possibilities. When people come into your home space, they should feel a solid confidence and not a rushed and fleeting chaos to your presence.

Right now, wherever you are, stand up. I want you to take a moment to be consciously aware of the heels of your feet. I want you to feel the connection of your heels to the floor. Gently lean back on your heels until you feel that you are firmly planted into the ground. While this may seem small, if physically and mentally you feel that you are on solid ground, you can extend that solid feeling to others when you shake their hand or hug them, when you extend a business card or share a thought. When people enter your home space, they need to feel as if you've got them, that you are solid and can be counted on, that there is a safe element about you.

Also in your home, you will easily kick-start conversations. Ask people about their journey, offer to take their coat, ask if they need anything, comment on the way they look, express your appreciation for their arrival, and so on. You will offer this small gift of 'chitchat' as an icebreaker to the more important conversations to come.

Now, in our digital age, many of our new connections may not be face to face, but some of these principles can still apply. Consider that your new connection is entering your home space, and your goal is to be hospitable and make it as comfortable for the other person as possible.

I am a big believer in sharing a photo or two in advance so that there is an increased sense of who you are. If the meeting is over a medium like Skype, I will always turn on my camera at the start and offer a smile and a wave even if I do not keep the camera on for the entire meeting. This is because when people come to my home, they see my face and feel my intention, so I want to convey this even if the experience is in an online setting.

Do not underestimate how important this is. Looking each other in the eyes, even in photos, is critical to the connection process.

Remember, you must always seek to generate emotional connections, and comfort is a very strong feeling for people. Also, you will find that because humans are wired with a reciprocity gene, the more you give of yourself and extend hospitality, the more other people will feel compelled to extend it back to you. Make creating comfort a sincere priority, and others will view you as open and inviting.

*H*ear with Your Eyes

We live in an age of distraction. We care more about what we want to do and what we want to look at, but positive human connectivity is about being all in. It is about making people feel valuable, respected, and heard. It is about being present in the moment. So my tip for you is to learn to consciously 'hear with your eyes.'

Please, this is not about staring someone down, nor is it even about holding constant eye contact. It is about training yourself to:

- Be aware of what your eyes are saying
- Focus on the precise words of the conversation
- Pick up key information stated by the other person that you can play into

If our eyes are our windows to our soul, why don't we have an elevated consciousness of what they are doing? People can pick up right away what our soul thinks, through our eyes. The eyes tell if we are listening, being authentic, or allowing our brains to wander somewhere further away. Take a moment to consider what your eyes are doing right now. Can you think and make your eyes be happy, understanding, thoughtful, sad, or angry? Often we give no thought to what our eyes are doing, but people can read our eyes and our intention very quickly.

Many believe effective networking is done face-to-face, building a rapport with someone by looking at them in the eye, leading to a solid connection and foundational trust. — *Raymond Arroyo, journalist, author, a man who proposes that as a society we can all do a little better than we are*

Seek to hear with your eyes, and then follow with your whole physical being. Listen to the words being spoken and seek to hear the stories and problems that are being shared. Do not underestimate how much people are driven to be understood and to be validated. Know that when you are actively listening, it is not your time to talk, but instead consider that you are a recording device and your objective is to reflect and restate what you have heard using different words. You can reflect the emotions expressed using phrases such as:

"It sounds as if that was difficult for you."

"I can sense how proud you are."

"I can feel your excitement."

Hearing with your eyes is like giving a gift of acceptance and inclusion to the other person.

Avoid Too Much Self

The problem with the elevator pitch is that the focus is all on you. It teaches you to lead with your own position and use your words, leading the other person. But consider there are times to be the mighty general and there are times to step back and be the humble foot soldier.

For most people it is contrary to their instincts to hold back. Each of us wants to be the one with the story. You want to go around telling others about your accomplishments, what you know, and the things you can do for other people. But be cautioned, people want to follow happy and successful people, but they also want to follow those who are not too full of themselves.

Think of importance versus purpose. This is not about showing others how important you are; it's about focusing on how you can be purposeful in the other person's eyes. It is about a collaborative conversation where there is at minimum equal airtime. Because of this, you may need to learn the skill of asking open-ended questions so that if you are across from an introvert you can delicately maneuver the conversation and not overwhelm.

The great American marketing guru Seth Godin has been quoted as saying, "It's a privilege to talk to people who will listen to you." He has been also known to say, "It is a gift if not a right to share your views."

I think these are great words to keep in mind as you are making new connections and balancing the ebb and flow of conversations. Make sure you are not giving too much of yourself but that you are allowing the other person to come forward into the spotlight as well.

What makes us human, I think, is an ability to ask questions, a consequence of our sophisticated spoken language.
—*Jane Goodall, primatologist, naturalist, UN Messenger of Peace, knows a bit about behavioral observation, social interactions, and primal instincts*

Relate Relevantly

If you have been able to create comfort, hear what is being said, and not consume the conversation, you will have been able to gain some solid information to begin to work with in order to relate relevantly to your connection. Keep three things in mind when relating relevantly: topic, timing, and word choice.

Make sure that whatever story you are about to tell or whatever business idea you are about to unveil means something to the person to whom you are speaking and in some way makes his own life happier, easier, richer, better connected, and more knowledgeable. The topic must be relatable for him. If you begin in a direction that is not getting a response or generating interest, adjust your sails, close the current points, and move in from a different angle.

When you get to the important moment, use your words wisely and speak in headlines because you don't know how much time you have before he disengages or switches topics on you. Think of the structure of a news article and the lead elements of who, what, when, where, and why.

Don't waste people's time by meandering through supporting details or rambling in unnecessary conversation. If you can't think in an organized manner and get to the point, you are taking too much of someone's time. Recognize when it is okay to chat for the sake of chatting versus chatting to the point of lost interest or reduced integrity. Time is a valuable commodity for the movers and shakers in the world; don't steal it from them.

Understand the value of your words and how to use them more effectively. If you pick up a copy of the book by Loretta Malandro, *Say It Right the First Time*, you will gain many valuable insights, as well as discover how to recover quickly when you fail. To seek more wisdom in this area, go to the book section of a source like Amazon and type in the search bar key phrases like 'say right' or 'say anything.'

Every now and then, you may get caught in a conversation where the person you are speaking with is expressing an opinion very different than your own. When you are building new relationships, it is not your role to conquer or force your views into the dialogue, but you do want to remain authentic to who you are.

Here are two handy phrases you can fall to in these situations. The first is: "That it's an interesting thought/view you have, but have you thought of it this way. . . ?" A second is: "I somewhat agree, but my experiences have led to a slightly different take on it." Of course an even more direct way out is: "I make it my policy not to talk politics (or whatever) when I am enjoying a nice conversation/glass of wine/meal." Once you have expressed your views, try to move the conversation in another direction rather than engaging on a topic that will undoubtedly reduce your position of trust and value.

If you get in a bind and don't feel you can relate relevantly, use the go-to phrase, "Tell me more." This opens the door for the other person to continue to share until you can find a point where you can contribute to the conversation.

Match Styles

It is human nature for people to be attracted to the familiar. Subconsciously, we want to be with people who are like us. Unknowingly, we self-select whom we approach, whom we smile at, whom we do favors for, whom we are more likely to say yes to, and so on. Familiar is easy.

Understanding this human need will help you become a stronger observer of the energy, mannerisms, and beliefs that the people we meet hold. While we need to be true to who we are, we must be aware of this underlying dynamic that is at play. We all want to be on what we perceive as level ground and meet in a common place. Even if the commonality is ever so small, our inner being will grab hold of it.

When you meet people, bring all the positivity you can bring but monitor your energy levels and physical responses. Consider that your goal is to become a mirror for the other person, to reflect back to him what he feels comfortable with.

Let me give you an example of imbalanced energy. A main mistake people with big personalities make is to push too much of themselves out there all the time. When traveling overseas I have seen it play out in a way that I call it the American cowboy syndrome. These people can be loud, dominate the conversation, shoot from the hip, and overwhelm the people around them, but they don't see it that way. They think they are bringing up the energy of the room, but others see them as attention hungry. This trait is not limited to Americans; bold personalities appear in all cultures in different ways. But if these people don't know how to balance their energy, they will actually limit their success. To even things out, these wonderful, lively personalities need to know how and when to take it down a notch in order to establish commonality and to get into a place of harmony. Then, as the relationship grows, each person can step more fully into who he/she is, but the unity has to come first.

On the flip side, there are people I consider as gentle koalas. They sit still, move slowly, and make few sounds, yet they are consumers of what is going on around them. The sad part is that rarely do businesspeople envision the koalas as leaders or partners. These quiet souls need to learn how to move up the energy scale even if all they are capable of is small bursts of conversations; they must learn to participate and contribute and must also seek to reach for commonality and harmony even if it takes them from their comfort zone.

Second to energy is physicality. Matching the physicality will bring you into the realm of familiar. Think of being a mirror, reflecting what you are seeing. Very, very subtly match the gestures and body stance of whom you are speaking to. If he places his hand on his chin, you place your hand on yours. If she is looking at something, you look in the same direction. If he is staying still, you stay still. Matching an individual in small ways that she can't really notice will help her soul feel like you are a similar soul.

But be cautioned. My intent is to help you know how to further build a feeling of comfort and deeper bonding, but some people teach modeling and neuro-linguistics programming (NLP) as a way of manipulating other people and tricking them. That is not my intent. My intent is to help you establish practices to open doors to new relationships that will evolve to long-term opportunities.

Matching styles is about observation and sensitivity. It is about minimizing barriers and crossing borders to give people the familiarity that they need to view you favorably.

Share Something of Value

People's lives are so complex and overburdened that we love when we are given the gift of something that we need. If you are capable of depositing even just one small valuable item with a person, you will become an everyday hero to him or her.

Being an everyday hero is important. It is not the big things in life that get most people down; it is the numerous small things. And if you can provide something of value, it just may mean that you are capable of doing it again and again, which in turn will build upon your brand position as a trusted resource.

Depending on the conversation or type of connection, the item could be as simple as a good laugh, a tip on a vacation spot, advice on a new app, insight into an industry process, or news from an article or blog you just read. If the opportunity and dialogue is deeper, it could be a business referral, linking good people together, or the promise to send interesting information along. The point to keep in mind is that you need to create a lasting impression through value-added conversations and actions.

Be aware, this may not be an easy task when you first start to practice it. But with a heightened awareness you can bring more and more ideas forward. Think of how often you may have had a nice conversation with someone, and all they did was follow up with their business brochure. Can't you learn to be a little more creative than that?

If you talked about travel or apps or sports, send the brochure but also send a link to an article or photo of interest. If you talked about problems in the workplace, search for and send an article on employee engagement. You must convey the belief that you offer value over obstacles, making you easy to work with.

Takeaways

☐ If you can give other people an experience that puts them at ease, they will remember you.

☐ If you can turn up your **CHARMS**, people will like you and want to work with you. Your mission is to:

Create a comfortable environment by always being the hostess.

Hear with your eyes so people have no doubt you are listening.

Avoid too much self and allow the other person to share his/her stories.

Relate relevantly and show respect and interest in the other person's experiences and values.

Match styles to play into human nature and laws of attraction.

Share something of value that will help the other person through new insights or information.

☐ Demonstrate that you are in the business of making things easy.

10

Win by Being User-friendly

Does it sound like tough work to collect information from someone you don't know and have no idea what he can offer? Do you find just the thought of such a task makes you feel awkward? Does the idea of approaching someone you don't know and striking a conversation overwhelm you?

If so, know you are not alone. Everyone who walks into a networking event by himself is hoping there will be someone there who will help make his time go smoothly. But there is good news. Most introverts can become more comfortable in the relationship-building process if they tap into the desire to make others comfortable or to fulfill their desire to gain facts and information. Extroverts may find that meeting new people and sharing stories is easy; however, they may not be so prepared to slow down, take the conversations one level deeper, and ask the right questions. In fact, hurried extroverts may cause other people to be uncomfortable. So everyone has something to learn here.

Don't presume that you are the only one in the room feeling stress. Only presume you have the power to rescue someone else from his or her own anxiety.

If you're nervous about approaching groups of people, one of the best tips I ever received was to approach groups of odd numbers of people, such as a group of three or five, and of course someone who is alone is easy to approach, too. When you do that it gives you an opportunity to speak to the odd person out, someone who is not as engulfed in the conversation, or one who feels on the edge of the conversation.

This doesn't mean that you need to be the life and soul of the party, or that you need to meet with everyone and crack a joke or two. It just means that if you focus on being user-friendly, making it easy for people to connect with you, they feel comfortable, which will help you become known as the person who makes doing business a pleasure.

Being user-friendly means you have developed the 'connection smarts' and interpersonal skills that accelerate ease of exchange—always your goal. But beware: you must be authentic in your exchange; superficial pleasantries will get you only so far without interest and empathy. As business leaders say, "You must be able to **be in the moment**."

Being user-friendly means that you will demonstrate respect and a willingness to care enough about the other person to make the exchange simple. You convey that you understand the fundamentals of relational communications.

Here are five traits that user-friendly people employ when meeting new people:
- Connect
- Contribute
- Consider
- Confide
- Don't conquer

Think about how you can utilize these best practices.

Connect

There is a physicality to connecting that is comprised of both verbal and nonverbal cues. Our minds comprehend what we see much faster than what we hear. And it is human nature that the second we come in contact with each other we measure facial expressions, body language, appearance, and perceived intent. This is because as humans we have a tribe mentality, and we are looking for cues that indicate the person before us is worthy of a place in our tribe. We are also seeing if there is a connection to the human spirit or the heart.

President Reagan achieved such successes because when you sat in a room with him, there could be over one thousand people in the room, yet you felt like there was only the two of you, and his wonderful wit would put you at ease. That was a tremendous gift. —*Elton Gallegly, devoted twenty-three years to the US House of Representatives fighting for the people of California, but also a champion of animals (whom he probably liked more in the end)*

And humans are clever. Even if the exchange is over the phone, we can tell if the tone and the words have a familiarity to them and if they feel authentic.

What about electronic formats like email?

I facilitated a roundtable in Germany about building stronger international partnerships, and my tip was "always send your photo to a new contact so that the exchange can be 'humanized.' " An American gal across from me expressed that she didn't have time for such things and did not see how that would help her job as a purchasing agent as numbers were all that interested her.

But she could not have been any more wrong. People you connect with want to know that either 1) there is something familiar about you that will allow you into the tribe, or 2) that you are appealing enough as a human that they might consider letting you in.

Showing your true humanity is a demonstration of respect for the person you wish to connect with because in this busy, hectic world you consider him or her worth your seeking to 'share a moment.'

Contribute

Always be willing to make the first move. People naturally see the world as revolving around them yet are often too cautious to offer the first smile or break the silence. Everyone yearns for inclusion, and you can give it to him or her. Feed others' sense of self-worth by contributing the first gesture of connection. Offer a warm greeting, a selfless smile, a hearty handshake, or a head bow. Be willing and have the courage to speak first.

In order to speak first you usually need to be prepared. Showing up and 'winging it' works in very few aspects of life. Have a list of questions that you already know before you walk in the room or pick up the phone. The most common topic when filling time is talking about the weather, but it is an utter waste of time. No one will think you are adding value because you are willing to share how cold/hot/rainy/snowy/stormy the day is.

Before you get on a phone call, write a few possible speaking points and questions. Before walking into a networking event, scribble some conversation starter topics based on your expected audience. For example, if you are going to a professional networking event, you could ask this string of questions:

- Is anything new going on in your business?
- By the way, how long have you been in your current role?
- What do you think the biggest change has been since you started?

- That must be a big job; do you still like it?
- Are your business goals tougher this year?

If you seek to enter a conversation asking open-ended questions, it will lead you to the next step, the ability to consider thoughtfully the response of the individual.

Consider

Being considerate to someone is a choice. It means you are thinking about that person and his or her needs first. To do this, focus on what the person is telling you by listening with your eyes and feeling with your ears. If you go to a traditional communication seminar, they will tell you that people don't listen because they are consumed with thinking about their own response. Actually, it is worse than that. Most people are simply just 'drunk with themselves.' What does that mean? Human beings like to hear themselves talk. They think by telling their own stories they are relating to other people. Actually, all they are doing is feeling good because they are satisfied with hearing themselves speak—and I know because I can be guilty of this. In fact, we all can.

Yes, you must learn to ask leading questions, but you must also learn how to listen. Be okay with moments of silence; don't feel you need to rush and control, moving along every moment of the conversation. Bring your hand to your chin, allow for a quiet smile and a head nod every now and then, and show you are processing what is being said to you. When you are really listening and considering what is being said to you, you are not rushing.

Going too fast tells the other person you are not really interested. When you have heard what the person has said, offer affirmation in small ways. Use phrases like:

- I never thought about it that way.

- That must be such a challenge.
- Wow, is that a big job.
- I give you credit.
- You should be proud.
- Thanks for sharing.

Your goal is to contribute and consider until you can understand that person's values and problems. When you can genuinely achieve that, you have constructed meaningful moments together.

Confide

There is nothing that can move a connection along faster than confiding in another person. After you have contributed and considered, try to share something about the way you feel in the moment. Tell him that you are nervous or that you don't know a single other soul in the room. Ask for help meeting other people in the room. Ask him for his opinion or views on a business situation. Ask her if you look okay. Offer an embarrassing story. Tell the person what your real need is and why you have shown up.

People are funny; the second you show some humility or ask for their advice, it puts them in a perceived position over you. And people like feeling that they are in a position over others. People also like secrets and learning about flaws —these make you memorable.

Go ahead and admit that your socks don't match, that you forgot someone's name, or that you need an outside opinion about a work matter. It is all about creating shared moments and giving the other person something to remember you by. Confiding in someone is depositing a small part of yourself for safekeeping, and most people are happy to be on the receiving end of that.

With practice you'll learn that confiding does not always mean you must share a deeply personal thing. It could be as simple as "I am looking for/need help with some new apps to make life easier. What do you have on your phone? Can you show it to me?"

Many people don't learn the art of confiding, such a loss. I would guess the lack stems from some leadership class where a speaker (who had never achieved the top levels of leadership himself) emphasized that to be a leader is to be an influencer, to charge ahead and have followers, and to display total confidence. I would argue that as a leader and connector you must allow people to see a small 'crack' every now and then as that is what makes you human and easier to relate to. Be approachable, not perfect. Be likeable, not superior.

One last point about why you should learn the art of confiding: humans have a mirror gene. The science of neuro-linguistics programming tells us that. We like other people to model their behaviors after us and we like to model behaviors after what we see. This is in our DNA because it is what helps us build a stronger tribe. Why, even when people see someone else sneeze, they must sneeze. So if you can learn to confide in others, eventually others will confide in you.

Don't Conquer

No one wants to be dominated or intimidated. The conversation should not be about you. No one wants to talk with someone who is a know-it-all. No one wants to hear all your success stories in a first encounter. Networking is not 'brag-working.' It is about sharing just the right balance of information so that you are of interest to the other person and even slightly intriguing. The only part of you that should come out in a first meeting is the friendly person who can offer interesting conversations and make known in a subtle

95

way how you can provide a business solution if it were ever to be needed by that individual or his/her company.

Don't be too loud, too funny, too pushy, too negative. Don't be 'too' anything other than considerate.

Being user-friendly means you know that when you seek to connect it is not about you. It is about your taking the lead but only as the dance partner who is seeking to bring out the best in the person you are choosing to dance with. People who are user-friendly do not bring drama and chaos to the table to get attention. They are not drunk on themselves or critical of others.

It's really important how you say things because people won't necessarily remember what words you used, but they'll remember how you made them feel. —*Brian McDermott, soccer player/coach/business manager, knows the joy of success and the realities of being sacked*

The human side of connecting is tough. Often we don't feel we are ready to be 'on' for another person. Sometimes when it is time to network and connect, we bring our own misperceptions, stress, bad attitudes, fears, and old experiences with us. But that is when we must reach deep down and rely on these learned skills of connecting. We must know how to contribute, consider, and confide. We must know not to be on a quest to conquer all conversation. We must show up as a professional, easily give away smiles, and seek to identify on a personal level.

A professional athlete can't just walk on a field and achieve peak performance without training, and neither can you. You must put yourself into more situations where you can consciously practice connecting on a human level.

Be User-friendly

Someone once said to me, "When you walk into a room, you must assume someone is having his best day ever and someone is having his worst day ever." Knowing this will make a difference in how you will approach them. Will you use either situation to make the person feel as positive about the encounter with you as possible? Will you employ the principle that 'you don't have to like someone to love him or her' across all your interactions?

While we speak in words, humans think in images and emotions. This is why after an encounter people will remember how you made them feel before they will remember the words you said. Remember above all things that a connection is a promise—a promise that you will accept, respect, and have a positive exchange with the person before you.

Takeaways

- [ ] You are not the only one who feels awkward or overwhelmed when it comes to connecting.
- [ ] Employ user-friendly tactics—connect, contribute, consider, confide, and don't conquer.
- [ ] Be as easy as matching point A to point A and point B to point B. Remember, people are intuitively attracted to easy.

11

Accelerate Executive Level Opportunities

Networking is an investment in your business. It takes time and when done correctly can yield great results for years to come. —Diane Helbig, *Author of* Lemonade Stand Selling, *believer in small-business power and preacher for accelerated growth*

The whole point of connecting is to gain a competitive advantage. Sure I can Google whatever I want, I can watch all the videos I desire, I can even get a university degree without having to speak to another soul. But this is all very one-sided. Even this book is one-sided, and in the moment I am writing this I wish I could be sitting in a room with you and enjoying a face-to-face exchange.

It is still and will always hold true that the information you gain from direct human-to-human conversations is more rich, authentic, meaningful, diverse, wise, and soul-stirring than anything you will receive from print, digital, social, film, or other media.

The process of exchange and collection is not one forced string of fitting in everything within two minutes of meeting someone. The goal is to convey a position of genuine curiosity that is very different from an interrogation of the person. Collecting information from other people is an art form so delicate that done right the other individual doesn't know you are slowly stealing knowledge, processing it, and then returning for more.

You need to see yourself as a connective curator who builds your personal museum of knowledge and wisdom. You must have an appetite for wisdom; you must know your goals and seek experts in many areas who will help you to achieve your goals.

As a collective curator, you can rely on the principle of **SPEED UP** to guide your business exchanges with both intention and focus:

Seek solutions
Plug into greater circles of influence
Expand business acumen
Envision the future
Diversify your point of view
Uncover executive traits
Permission to engage

Seek Solutions

One of the best strategies I have learned in business is to ask myself, "What problem am I trying to solve here?" At every stage of our business and professional life, we have different needs and face different challenges. That one question can frame so many things and lead to more tangible and relevant questions.

Often we find ourselves trying to solve the wrong problem or spinning our wheels in the wrong direction simply because we are not placing enough focus on conscious thought about what could make our life easier if we had the right answer.

If I had only one hour to save the world, I would spend fifty-five minutes defining the problem, and only five minutes finding the solution. —*Albert Einstein, theoretical physicist, poster boy for smart people of the world*

Why would you want to make your journey to success any longer than it needs to be? You need to embrace the practice of recognizing your challenges and hold an intention for securing a solution. Because I maintain a heightened awareness of my challenges, I can quickly navigate a conversation to finding solutions. Sometimes the solution comes and sometimes it doesn't, but even when it doesn't, the dialogue still gets me one step ahead of where I was.

When you go to a networking event, consider that it is not only to meet people but that it is to help you seek a solution. Think of it as your own crowdsourcing. Think before you walk in the room about whom you hope to meet and what you hope to achieve. Consider: what does success look like? Imagine that success, and be thankful for it in advance.

For example, in the past few weeks I have had a few different challenges I was working on. So at my networking events, meetings, and social gatherings, I worked these challenges into conversations. Here are just a few:

- I was interested in social media platforms used in Asia to increase communication avenues. Asking my contacts, I learned people use Line and Viber. The next week I opened a Line account and began connecting.
- I needed a freelance learning management system professional. I met an ex-coworker who referred me to a

community group website I wasn't aware of as well as provided a name to connect to on LinkedIn.

♦ I was seeking affirmation that I had handled a difficult employee issue with the correct tact. At a dinner party I had a great visit with two ladies who, as childcare center directors, had dealt with similar issues. While they were from a completely different industry, the discussion was well worth my time.

It doesn't matter how big or small your challenge is or what you want to learn. What matters is that you are consciously aware of the things you need and that you are willing to work those items into conversations. I could have been looking for anything—to get connected to a person, to find a better solution for transfer of monies, or to locate a new web commerce partner. The point is to hold an acute awareness of what you need and work it into conversations.

And you know what? When you ask people for a favor or for advice, they remember that, and based on the way we are wound as humans, it endears you to them. So often we are too shy or intimidated to ask for advice, but when you make another person feel valued, he feels good and equates that good feeling with you.

So ask and you shall receive. When you connect, seek to collect solutions to your problems because seeking shortcuts to solve your problems will help you in business and in life. Someone else has already solved the problem, so why should you spend time and energy only to get to the same point? I am trained and disciplined to focus on what it is that I need, and I am willing to put the question out there and ask. You need to do the same.

I even recommend that you ask your network for advice every now and then even if you don't need an answer. Simple questions let you stay connected.

*P*lug into Greater Circles of Influence

You must know people more connected than yourself because your connections are a predictor of your future success. But when you walk into a room, do you know how to identify these people? Do you know just by looking around who holds the money, the knowledge, and the influential connections? And are you willing to walk up to them and strike up a conversation or offer a compliment?

Part of the discovery process is quickly figuring out how a new person you are meeting is connected and if those connections will be of any value to you. This comes back to sizing up the opportunity when you meet people and placing them in 'the moment, the maybe, or the must' category.

The choices we make dictate the lives we lead. —William Shakespeare, master observer of people, power, and influence and chap who was quite good with a pen

---

When connecting into greater circles of influence, you are seeking business owners, executives, and people whom you believe have a positive swagger and intelligence that attracts other influential people. You can weave into conversations questions about business, hobbies, and membership organizations to ascertain how highly connected they are and if their circle is one of which you want to be a part. But remember, people of influence will also be evaluating you.

Many times you will walk into a setting already knowing who the big dogs are whom you want to get close to. For this, I want to share a secret with you. Most people at the top are just as lonely and feel just as awkward as the people at the bottom. Sure, there are arrogant snobs and people who won't have time for you, but some of that is also just a wall of protection to shield them from feeling scrutinized or having too many people ask for things of them.

But in the end, know that the big dogs like a compliment and an intelligent question from someone who is not seeking anything immediately in return. The big dogs do crave a genuine conversation as a human first and then as business leaders second. To attract the big dogs you need to be brave, make them feel comfortable, and connect into what is important to them.

Let me share a few examples:

Story One—Be Brave and Engage

When I joined the staff at a large publicly traded US company in a director level role, I was fortunate enough to be invited to a roundtable session with the CEO. When the seriousness of the session was complete, in a moment of small conversation, he shared that being the CEO was tough because people could be intimidated and stay away from him. He expressed that people didn't naturally come sit with him because they either didn't know the protocol or were scared. In fact, he shared that he always felt better when someone would join him at a lunch table or walk up to talk to him at a company event. He didn't like to be the lonely CEO.

I found this to be very insightful. The CEO feeling alone? The concept had never crossed my mind. From that point, I always made sure to feel very comfortable walking up to him at any event with outstretched hand for a good solid shake hello.

But it didn't end with him. Even after that I have made sure that I give the people at the top the right level of respect, but I never shy away from engaging with them.

Story Two—Make It Comfortable

As the executive director of an international association in the MICE space (meetings, incentives, congresses, and
events), I attended many trade shows. At one event I was
walking the trade-show floor with my past president. He was
an impressive man leading a global company that was expanding at a rapid rate. His financial status and influence were
well known. Throughout the day, people would come up and
say hello, and as they walked away, he would tell me what
they really wanted: a new job, a business partnership, an investment, and so on. So I began to listen to the people, and I
noticed that these conversations moved too abruptly to what
they wanted without first connecting on a human level.

In my role, I didn't want anything; I was just walking
with him. It was then I realized my value to him, and my win-
ning position was in making him comfortable. I offered honest conversation, praise about his business, and questions that
held a genuine curiosity.

If you want to gain wisdom as well as respect from top
leaders in business, make them comfortable.

**Story Three—Connect into
What Is Important for Them**

A business friend had the opportunity to attend an
event where Michael Eisner, former CEO of The Walt Disney
Company, would be present, and he really wanted the chance
to speak with him. The only problem was there would be
hundreds of people at the same event. So beforehand he took
the time to read Michael Eisner's book *Camp*. Going through
a reception line he had only a brief moment to say hello and
make a connection, and in that moment he chose wisely to
make a personal statement that connected to the book. Later

that evening, Michael Eisner found his way back to my friend, and they had a relevant one-to-one conversation about youthful camp experiences and leadership lessons. By connecting into Mr. Eisner's passion, my friend had opened an opportunity to engage in a personal conversation with one of the most influential business leaders of our time. I can only say I wish it had been me.

Know that when you seek to plug into greater circles of influences you may gain contacts or you may gain wisdom. But either way you most certainly will have gained something that you didn't have before.

*E*xpand Business Acumen

Advanced college degrees are nice and can provide tremendous insight into business theories and systems, but they are certainly not a guaranteed path to success (just ask all the unemployed people with master's degrees). A predictor of success is how well you display and apply your business acumen to future employers, customers, and business partners.

Education, associations, and business publications are great ways to build knowledge, but you must learn to absorb all you observe through your connections and exchanges. You must seek to learn from people who own the businesses or hold the positions above yours that you want to step into. They have vital information you need.

Think about connective channels to which you can turn to find new connections and people who are at a higher level in business than you so you can observe the business language that they use.

Consider doing an evaluation of how well you know the following areas of business. Rate yourself on a scale of 1 to 10 with 1 being the lowest and 10 being the highest. What is your level of business acumen for each?

Accelerate Opportunities

Business Expertise	Rating
Board & shareholder relations	
Budget development	
Business plan development	
Call center management	
Capacity/efficiency management	
CRM (customer relationship management)	
Customer acquisition	
Database management	
Digital media	
Finance	
Human resources	
Insurance coverage and policies	
Investment accounts	
IT management	
Labor relations	
Lead generation	
Legal counsel	
Marketing	
Monthly financial statement review	
P&L (profit & loss) estimates	
Procurement and purchasing	
Project management	
Proposal & contract development	
Public relations	
Order fulfillment	
Operations management	
Risk management	
Strategic selling	
Transportation	
Warehouse management	
Supervision of direct reports	
Website development	
Some other area I know absolutely nothing about:	

The above list can be overwhelming even for people with years of diverse business experience, but this list can be particularly tough for an individual who has entered his/her career in a professional specialty. For example, if you have trained to be a nurse or software developer, you likely did not have a lot of general business courses on your way to where you are. But to take the next step—to move into leadership, become a consultant, start your own business—you must expand your business acumen.

If you want the people you work for to see you the right way, you must be able to hold an informed conversation. If you want to be an entrepreneur and establish a business, you must recognize what you don't know and figure out how to bridge the gap in knowledge. Sure, you can move into management or start a business without knowing all of the above, but you are guaranteed to be in the business of learning from your mistakes rather than gaining wisdom from those who have gone before you.

I doubt most people think about this, and do you know where that leaves them? **Unprepared!**

To move up and grab the next level—to be equipped to jump from a five-figure income to a six-figure income— you must strengthen your all-around business knowledge. You must begin to learn how money is made from the front door to the back door of the enterprise. This is why you must value collecting knowledge from people who work in areas very different from your own.

Envision the Future

Once upon a time Kodak and Polaroid were leaders in the film industry. The public's demand for cameras and print photos was a booming global industry for a century. Then the world changed. Telephones got cameras. Then the world changed again. We shared photos over the internet or direct phone to phone. We embraced Facebook and Instagram and other apps that let us shoot images around the world in split seconds. And we could go online and purchase other photographers' images or download license-free images with the ease of a click of a mouse. While the camera industry still exists and people still print photos, the industry that was on top only twenty years ago has dwindled so much in size that few would think about investing their hard-earned dollars in a company that makes cameras or sells film.

Today the world is changing, and it is changing rapidly. When my daughter was in college she was incredibly intimidated at the prospect of selecting her major. I told her not to worry because I was sure that the job she would have in the future was a job that didn't even exist at that time. I thought I was being helpful, but instead I doubled her anxiety. But it is the current state of things.

Do any of you remember when the internet was dial-up and you had to know basic DOS commands to navigate anywhere? I even remember sitting in my first lecture on this new thing called Twitter, where it was introduced as a way to say good morning to all your friends in your circle at the same time. That was it; Twitter was only useful to send a single message to people in your group. In no way could I ever have imagined that Twitter would later have such a huge role in the business world.

But Twitter wasn't the only place that saw capitalism as an early adapter. Nike is credited with creating the first YouTube video that attempted to sell a product without formatting itself as a commercial. Who knew these things would evolve in the way they did?

In the future the world will change, and it will change rapidly. You cannot depend on trends to come across in the headlines. By the time the news reaches headlines, the old normal has already been altered. In 2001, I worked in the trade-show industry, and we could see by our revenues that a recession was coming. We knew it before many of the economists were declaring it because we had already felt it in the way exhibitors had pulled back their footprints and budgets on the trade-show floor.

I also remember the first time I heard of a 3D printer. Crazy good stuff. I was at a conference in Antwerp, and a futurist gave a presentation on how the future was already here. But it wasn't only about the 3D printer; he also showed how you could print food and warned us of the impact of the sharing economy. Again, who could have understood a thing like Uber or Airbnb?

Being connected to the right people can help you view what is coming on the horizon before it has fully arrived. It will help you prepare for better or worse. It will cause you to think if you need to make any adjustments in your career or prepare for the way your business will be changed.

Ask people you meet about the health of their business, about new products or services they are working on, if they are expanding or holding tight. Find out what clues you can about the direction of tomorrow. Connect into marketers and social media experts as they also watch trends and seek to be early adapters. Everyone should have a good marketer among their closest of friends as marketers often transverse multiple areas of business.

Here, it is important not only to gather what you can in face-to-face interactions but also to look up futurists to follow through blogs or Twitter. Keep your mind open when reading business publications for insights into the next new.

The future will bring change, and we can choose to run alongside it or it can knock us right over if we stand still. Gain the information you need to run in the right direction.

Change is the law of life. And those who look only to the past or present are certain to miss the future. —*John F. Kennedy, thirty-fifth US President and visionary who publicly committed to putting a man on the moon by the end of the 1960s with no capable spacecraft, no rocket powerful enough, no plan how to land it, and no idea how to get it home*

Diversify Your Point of View

In a world that has delivered us near instantaneous methods of communications, it sometimes seems as if our differences are greater than ever. The ease of migration has moved people further from their birth homes and resulted in more multi-cultural communities and a need to transverse language barriers and cultural divides. The evolution of technology has created significant shifts in the way each generation interacts with the world.

The rifts in the economy have stifled opportunity and broken down beliefs in governments. Human interaction has been removed from many processes as people can order goods and services without stepping outside their homes or having a live conversation.

There is no such thing as one size fits all any more— now one size fits no one. For this reason, you must learn to look outside yourself and understand other points of view because your coworkers and customers will likely not look like you or think like you. And they most certainly will not buy like you.

Becoming an observer of people and gaining alternate points of view will lead you to smarter word choices and an increased ability to mirror basic cultural behaviors. When you enter a room, try not to take what you consider to be the safe route of walking up to someone who looks like you. Dig into your brave side and choose to connect with an individual who is opposite you in age and culture. You can still embrace the practices we have discussed in this book but with the added dimension of watching and adapting as appropriate.

While in America we live in a society that values political correctness, don't be afraid to venture underground and ask slightly intrusive questions; after all, the underground is so much more interesting than the surface. While timing and tact are everything, most people are happy to share their culture and point of view. Sometimes what you think is strange and should be embarrassing is not at all embarrassing for the other person. I had a most engaging and insightful conversation with a business associate from China about communism, the one-child policy, and what I perceived as other social ills. To my surprise, she had no concern answering questions since she wanted me to hear the topics from her point of view.

Seek first to understand, then to be understood. —*Stephen R. Covey, global leadership expert, educator, and author who taught the world how to be highly effective*

The message here is be confident in somebody's desire to respond and confide in you. You just may find that people will tell a complete stranger things they won't even tell someone whom they know, so take advantage of it. Of course if they don't want to respond, just redirect the conversation.

As you are seeking to expand your point of view, you must consider suspending judgment. Recently, I was in a conversation with a group of managers who were expressing frustration with the incoming group of college graduates. After listening for a while, I interjected two questions. The first was: "What have you done to adapt to their communication needs?" and the second was: "Have you ever considered there are things they don't do simply because no one has taken the time to discuss it with them and show them how?"

Thinking and interacting across generations and cultures will serve you well on your journey. Don't confuse my call for an open mind as a request to change who you are or the core values that you hold, but it will demonstrate that you can see the world in broader terms and therefore react differently than the business professionals who wish to remain closed to the possibilities that thinking differently can hold. Take time to pause and think before saying "no" or jumping in with your own view or solution. If you are young in your professional life, seek to understand your bosses. If you are mature in your professional life, seek to understand the new up-and-coming leaders who are behind you. Diversifying your point of view will most certainly expand the way you build teams, solve problems, and take products to market.

Uncover Executive Traits

Executives have a cultural way of their own, and when they are selecting partners or thinking about promotions, they are looking for people who will best fit into their own culture. Even venture capitalists recognize that they are investing in people as much as they are investing in products and services. If you view yourself as 'executive material,' you must be sure others can view you that way as well.

I have mentored many employees who don't know why they can't make the step up. The answer is simple: they fail to realize that the skills that got them where they are now are not the same skills they need for the next level. They don't understand that passing through each level requires an evolution of who they are, how they think, and how they present themselves. They can't see that business has a different language—both spoken and unspoken—at each level. Most of all, they can't see how the executives ahead of them have been molded through years of demanding decisions and accountability for business plans, payroll, sales goals, customer retention, and more. But these things can be seen if you earnestly look for them.

Consider famous entrepreneur Daymond John, who grew up in Queens, NY, and started selling his billion-dollar brand FUBU in the streets. To see Mr. John today, you would recognize him as a work of professional perfection in both mannerisms and presence. He most certainly evolved as his business world evolved, and so must you.

People who get positional and think they have the right stuff 'as is' will have a tough time achieving the success they desire and think they deserve. The smart people, the individuals who want to get to the top quickly, will seek out proper role models. They will plan to show up at places and at times where they have the best chance to meet executives. They will observe how they dress, how they hold themselves, whom they are interested in speaking to, and whom they are dismissive of. They will figure out what these business leaders are reading and to whom they are listening. Smart people will figure out how to observe and adapt their way to the top. Even Mark Zuckerberg knows when a great suit is needed.

The questions you will ask when connecting to a C-suite executive will be different than those asked of other professionals. The CEOs and CFOs of the world have thick skin, they have become experts at stress and getting yelled at, and they know what it's like to shoulder the burden for the team, to work more hours than anyone else, to manage hopeless budgets, to deal with government regulations, and to face other tough realities. But remember, you are going to take them to a place of comfort. You understand that top executives are driven by pride and accomplishment, and you can tap into those motives.

A great place to connect with an executive in a conversation is the topic of travel. Today's executives are usually well traveled and have vacationed in remarkable places, so they are happy to share bragging rights. Of course, you can also get an executive talking if you ask her to share the career paths she took to get her where she is.

Your role when connecting with executives is to be open and coachable in every moment. You must maintain a growth perspective in order to support you in finding your own leadership voice and style. Adopting the right style will convey professional effectiveness and foster trust with leaders in your industry.

If you fail to uncover the traits of executives, you may end up in a holding pattern. This will most definitely limit the places that you may land in the future.

Permission to Engage

The final and most important part of the SPEED UP collection philosophy is to gain permission to engage. Remember, you are seeking constructive connections to help you in the future. Do not feel pressured to connect with everyone, but instead connect with intention. Many conversations end up being just for what you can gain 'in the moment,' and it is good to recognize that.

You can certainly enjoy an exchange and walk away from it, but if you feel the connection is in 'the must' category, you need to make the move to:
1. exchange data and
2. agree on a commitment to an action.

How do you seek permission to connect? This is more than just exchanging a business card because it is protocol. It is opening a door to talk again in the future.

Come up with a few phrases you can be comfortable with. This will help reduce the pressure in the moment. The more you prepare to connect, the easier this becomes.

Some examples are:

- I know our conversation was short, but I was interested in what you shared. If it's okay, may I come back to you as a resource in the future?
- I don't know if I can ever help you, but if we connect on LinkedIn you can reach out to me if I can do anything for you in the future.
- Just in case I forgot what you said about that (app, company, information, destination, etc.), can we connect on LinkedIn so I can come back to you if needed?
- I am happy to share my contact information, and I will send you a note if I plan to come to another event because I enjoyed talking with you.
- There is someone I would like to connect you to/information I would like to share with you/etc., so if you share your details with me, I will send it to you.
- Here's my card. I always make it a point to connect with other (sports team) fans or other lovers of (wine, travel, marathons, etc.).

Notice in the above examples there is not a direct question trying to close a sale. Unless the person you have spoken with is inviting a sales meeting, don't push for one. In your follow-up message, you can let him/her know that your services are available if needed. The point is first to be connected, second to be human, and third to show the value you hold in solving problems whether it be through your professional knowledge or the services you are selling. People remember people they like, and people will remain connected to people they think will help them.

What If You Can't Get Permission to Connect?

There will be people in your 'must' category who will not make the move to share information at the time you meet them. This may not always be a direct reflection on you; it may be that they don't want to share their details with other individuals who are also nearby. Therefore, no one gets the information. In this instance you must do a little research and send a follow-up note through Twitter, LinkedIn, their corporate email, etc. In the follow-up, you need to reconnect to something of interest that you enjoyed talking about and extend an invitation to connect.

The point I want you to take away here is you should feel confident to go after the permission to engage and exchange information, but don't be disappointed if it does not work out the way that you hope. Odds are you did nothing wrong; there just may be something else that is off.

Other times, especially with more powerful businesspeople, you will have to work to meet the individual a few times before he/she will be open to building a relationship. This can be because your first connections weren't the right timing. It could be because the person stays very private. It could be because he thinks you want to make a big ask of him. Just because you meet someone and don't get the permission the first time, don't give up.

I met one CEO at two different conferences, but it wasn't until I participated in the same golf outing that I stepped into a position where he valued my contributions. Now I know he will take a call from me, which is much more important than any digital connection. I also know another CEO whom I had met at different times over six years, including sitting on both an industry board and coalition with him, and he still has no clue who I am when I see him at conferences. To that I say it is his loss, not mine.

Takeaways

- ☐ Think about your new potential connections before you walk into a room. Consider whom you hope to meet and what you hope to achieve.
- ☐ Wisdom is more vital than information. Understanding how to apply the knowledge you have in real-life application becomes wisdom, and that's what a well-developed network is going to give you.
- ☐ Use the principles of the **SPEED UP** philosophy to help you connect and build wisdom:
  Seek solutions
  Plug into greater circles of influence
  Expand business acumen
  Envision the future
  Diversify your point of view
  Uncover executive traits
  Permission to engage

12

Gain the Ultimate Influence: Trust

Early in this book we talked about influence coming from position, knowledge, character, reputation, and network. Now we are talking about holding the ultimate influence through trust. I believe this is the rarest type of influence, so once you have it, cherish and honor it.

If people like you they'll listen to you, but if they trust you they'll do business with you. —Zig Ziglar, *tenth of twelve children, learned to motivate and sell to others to get ahead in life (and probably to get food at the table while growing up)*

Trust is a very delicate thing. Think about it; without trust you can't have betrayal. And why is that? It is because trust resides at the deepest level of influence. Trust is deeply rooted in emotions because trust is something that you permit someone to enjoy.

At the point of trust, you have the intersection of:
♦ Shared experiences
♦ Reliability and dependability
♦ Honesty and truth
♦ Proven abilities and knowledge
♦ Unspoken social protection

Becoming a trusted resource is more than being a resource for knowledge. A trusted resource is valued for his or her opinion, integrity, and often the ability to get specific jobs done. Therefore, you can't simply gain trust by writing blogs or sending sales emails; you must get into the human space. You must develop relationships.

Mutual trust means that two people will look out for each other's interests and welfare, that there is a predictability regarding actions and outcomes and an accountability to one another. The trust means the two can have a confidence level greater than in general transactions. To quote our friend Mr. Covey again, "When the trust account is high, communication is easy, instant, and effective."

But there are legal laws around trust and human laws around trust, and breaking either will get you in trouble.

It takes twenty years to build a reputation and five minutes to ruin it. —*Warren Buffett, chairman and main shareholder in Berkshire Hathaway, ukulele playing, once door-to-door salesman who through mastering investments grew to being known as one of the wealthiest men in the world—and definitely an individual who knows about trust*

If you can develop trust in business, it will do wonderful things for you. Once I made a mistake in estimating the expense of flooring for an event, and that mistake was going to cost about ten thousand dollars. Fortunately, I was able to contact our flooring partner and explain I misread the floor plans. Because I was a trusted client, they rushed the additional flooring on a truck cross-country and charged me only for the transportation and raw materials. Thus, they helped me get my mistake down to just under three thousand dollars so that when I told my boss it was at least an improved situation. But trust has brought me so much more—opportunities, relationships, increased earnings, and many other benefits.

Trust makes people want to please and support you. It makes gaining consensus easier and helps encourage others to follow when uncertainty and doubt might otherwise be tugging at their hearts.

A book to pick up on the topic is *The Trusted Advisor*, which focuses on what trust is, how to build trust, and how to put trust to work. One of the authors, Charles H. Green, has stated, "It takes two to do the trust tango—the one who risks (the trustor) and the one who is trustworthy (the trustee); each must play their role." The book holds wisdom about how you can shift from transactional relationships into the role of a trusted advisor. And this is the sweet spot in terms of business influence, the place where people seek you out and then accept and adapt to your views and guidance.

Take some time to think about what trust means to you. Whom do you trust? Why do you trust them? Who trusts you? What have you done to deserve that trust? Is there someone to whom you should give more trust?

Trust is the highest form of human motivation. It brings out the very best in people. —Stephen R. Covey, so good I just had to quote again. . . .

Takeaways

☐ Trust is the ultimate component of influence and is more likely to motivate people than anything else.

Connect to Influence

☐ Trust will bring you opportunities, new business, and respect.
☐ Trust lost is hard to regain.

13

Avoid Networking Mistakes

Welcome to chapter 13. I am glad you are still here! It is great that you understand the value of being highly connected, you know where you stand today, and you are designing a vision for where you want to go and how you will show up to give a great impression, but this seems like a good place to pause and consider the behaviors that you need to avoid or figure out how to overcome.

When it comes to networking, there are several very simple do's and do not's, and many of them are common sense. Unfortunately, common sense is not always the same as common practice, particularly in business circles. Following are twenty-one of the most common networking mistakes that people make.

1. **Network in the wrong places.**
   It's great that you are getting out there and networking, but if you are not meeting the people who can add value to your network, you have been networking in the wrong places. No matter how many of the wrong conections you may have, they will not improve your overall Connective Health Score. Once you spend time, you can never get it back, so network in the places where you will get a positive return on the time you have invested.

2. **Fail to follow up.**

   Once you make a connection, the follow-up is what helps to build the relationship. Over 50 percent of people never follow up, so even just saying thank you is going to make you memorable. And keep the first follow-up correspondence personable and friendly; hold any sales pitches for the next time.

3. **Think you already know everyone.**

   Don't want to go to an event because you think you will see the same people you already know? Then make it a goal to go deeper. Just because you think you know someone, that's not the same as knowing who he or she is on a deeper level and whom he/she knows. You are not just looking to add people to your network, but you want to connect to the networks of other people as well.

4. **Focus on the result, not the relationship.**

   Patience is a virtue that pays off in networking; we need to focus on building the relationship. When we do that, there's a good chance that the results we are looking for will come. If we focus on the result, we will never build a strong relationship. Again, personable and friendly first.

5. **Talk to too many people.**

   Networking isn't a numbers game. It's not about who can collect the most business cards. Being perceived as a shallow serial networker is not going to enhance your reputation.

6. **Talk to too few people.**

   While we need to spend time getting to know people,

do not get trapped speaking to one person all evening. Give yourself the opportunity to meet at least three or four people per half-hour of networking time.

7. **Be inauthentic.**

Authenticity builds trust, and people are more likely to recommend and do business with the people they trust. Authentic people listen to others and respond on point. This is where introverts can really excel and the overtalkative extroverts can miss the mark.

8. **Fail to be well prepared.**

You never know when the right opportunity is going to present itself, and there is nothing worse than not knowing what to say or ask when that moment arrives. Poor preparation will not get you the results you are looking for. Gain information in advance of the event on such details as attendees and the speakers. Know who may be in the room whom you want to know.

9. **Arrive uninformed.**

You need to be up to date with your industry or the industry of the person with whom you are hoping to build a relationship. Few things are more embarrassing than being asked about the biggest change in your area of business and having to say, "I didn't know about that."

10. **Make it all about you.**

The best relationships are built based on 'give and take,' and when you make them all about you, you violate this golden rule. During the conversation, make sure that you ask at least as many questions as you are asked and actively listen to the responses.

125

11. **You are rude.**

Whether you are rude to the person you are looking to connect with or to the waiter who has forgotten your drink for the second time, an inconsiderate attitude will affect your image negatively. Rudeness is not an attractive quality when it comes to building relationships, and people always remember the ugly.

12. **Incorrectly assess the value of the connection.**

While it's true that all that glitters is not gold, the reverse is also true. Just because a person isn't shining doesn't mean that he/she is not a great connection. In fact, many CEOs are quite bad at networking and can stand alone just waiting to be spoken to. Also, we never know who knows whom. Make sure you understand not only the individual but also his network. Otherwise, you could overlook a fantastic connection.

13. **Forget the thank you.**

Common courtesy will take you a long way; however, its absence can stop you in your tracks. "Thank you" are two words which cost nothing to give but for which the return can be immeasurable.

14. **Interrupt conversations.**

Whether you are interrupting an ongoing conversation in order to join in or interrupting the person to whom you are speaking, it sends a very bad signal. We need to show respect. Give people the opportunity to have their say or wait to be invited to join a conversation. To 'butt in' shows you to be selfish and self-centered.

15. **Push the 'hard sell.'**

No one comes to a networking event to be sold to and

nothing turns people off quicker than being delivered the hard sell. Trying to persuade someone to buy a service they neither want nor need in the wrong moment will forever lose the contact.

16. Complain.
Positive people attract positive people and positive results. Complaining is negative, and few people want to add negative components into their networks. No one needs to know what went wrong in your day. A networking moment should be happy and carefree.

17. Overindulgence in alcohol.
There is nothing wrong with having a drink, but you need to make sure that you drink in moderation (and observe the practices of those to whom you wish to connect). Do not put yourself in a position where you may end up saying things that you later regret.

18. Criticize someone not present.
When we criticize people who are not present, we are telling much more about ourselves than we are about those we are criticizing. This behavior also sends the message that we are willing to badmouth other people behind their backs, which is not a good way to win friends or influence people. The people we are talking to know that if we can publicly criticize someone else, we can potentially do the same to them in the future.

19. Miss the personal point of pain.
The more we know about our connections, the better we can understand and serve their needs. There may be something very simple we can do that would make a significant difference to them. After all, everyone

falls short in some way in his business life, but without learning about his goals and challenges, we can miss the opportunity to put forward a recommendation that could be the answer he is looking for.

20. **Capture the contact details.**
There is nothing more frustrating than meeting a perfect connection only to discover later that you do not have contact details. Not having contact details available is the same as not having met that person at all.

And the biggest of all the mistakes that people make when it comes to networking?

21. **Fail to show up.**
That's right. Many people register for events or make plans to meet but opt out at the last minute. You may talk yourself out of it, stay at work longer, sit on your couch, convince yourself it's not worth the effort, or say you don't feel up to it. But you must make deposits into your account for your future career; you have to get up and head out to build your network.

Takeaways

☐ Make common sense your common practice.
☐ Be positive, polite, friendly, and helpful as the most memorable connections come from authentic conversations that connect on an emotional level.
☐ Make sure you keep contact details, follow up, and start to build a strong relationship.

14

Manage Distractors to Success

There is no journey worth taking that is not plagued with challenges, and your journey will be no different. Even after you have carefully established your connection goals, defined a bold strategy, and stepped onto a path designed to consciously collect knowledge and wisdom to enhance your life's opportunities, you will hit obstacles.

Obstacles don't have to stop you. If you run into a wall, don't turn around and give up. Figure out how to climb it, go through it, or work around it. —Michael Jordan, Olympian, basketball superstar, and business leader known to reflect a 'Just Do It' attitude

---

It is inevitable that you will have situations come up that demand your attention, and you will have people's uninvited views play with your mind and drain your energy. But your priority must be to embrace the fact that you do not want to settle for an ordinary life. You must keep your intentions clear for the universe, and you must believe that you have a right to the destination that is waiting for you.

You must be on guard against the things that will cause you to lose speed. I come from Chicago—the city of big shoulders—and when I feel like I am slowing down or that I am reaching for more than I have a right to, I fall back to this quote on big thinking:

Make no little plans; they have no magic to stir men's blood and probably themselves will not be realized. Make big plans; aim high in hope and work, remembering that a noble, logical diagram once recorded will never die, but long after we are gone will be a living thing, asserting itself with ever-growing insistency. —Daniel Burnham, *father of the modern skyscraper and visionary for urban design*

You have the right to execute your dreams, and you have a right to build something beyond your present-day circumstance. But keeping your heart and your head fueled and engaged on your long journey may be tough, so think about the deterrents that will come your way as they will likely fall in one of four categories:

- Time thieves
- Brain bandits
- Energy marauders
- Practical pirates

Time Thieves

We all have the same amount of time, but how you choose to use your time on a daily basis will propel you forward. You must protect your time and beware of time lost and time stolen.

Time lost is within your control. Think of your day as building blocks of time. From a high-level perspective, you can identify the time you must give to required tasks, time that you do not have much control over. Then you have time that you fill with things you need to do, but your preparation and actions may determine how much time you expend. Perhaps you can find efficiencies here, or maybe you can't.

Finally, there is the flexible time, the time you get to choose where you place your focus. There are great activities that fill this space—exercise, family events, and so on—but then there are things that seduce your time and attention away from forward momentum.

The worst is the seduction of the couch, where you spend mindless time watching TV, gaming, or tapping away on computers and tablets. Scanning and clicking through social media, attractive videos and photos, and other mindless online content will steal minutes—no, hours—from your life, and you know it.

Remember what gets measured gets mastered. Build in time for activities that you enjoy but also monitor that time and ensure that you do not sacrifice your dreams of tomorrow as you do. Learn how to set the fifteen-minute timer on your phone alarm so that when you say you want to be mindless for only fifteen minutes, you can really keep track of those precious minutes.

The toughest time to manage is when others begin to schedule your time for you. Your company has a new project that extends your already hectic schedule. Your family has projects and special events that require your presence. Your kids need to be shuttled places; they need help with homework and gluing together school projects. Your mom will get locked out of her computer again, and your dog will do something shameful. From important to frivolous, every demand takes time.

Time thieves have no respect for your time; they only have respect for their jobs that they believe must be done and the obligations that they believe should be your priority. This

131

challenge can become very tough to manage, and your options may be limited.

When I think of things that steal my time, I look it at three ways: can I do it with ease, can I do it with money, or can I do it with limitations? I don't say no to simple things that I can do with ease and get 'credit' for. I may even consider if, in what I am being asked to do, I can contribute with money instead. Of course, this may not always be possible (or make people happy), but it may be an option. Or I may determine if I can do it with set limitations. In other words, I will establish how much time I can give and when I can give it, or I will ask what can be left undone or sacrificed in order to fit in the tasks that I really want to invest my time in. Sometimes you need to know your 80 percent is just as good if not better than other people's 100 percent as long as you are focused when you are in the moment.

We can't stop the time thieves from coming, but we can recognize them and contain them as best we can.

In all our deeds, the proper value and respect for time determines success or failure. —Malcolm X, *human rights activist who knew what it was like to live on borrowed time yet still work tirelessly for what he believed in*

Brain Bandits

If you are smart and driven to succeed, I am sure brain bandits come after you frequently. These are the people who look for your help in a multitude of situations. They have learned to deliver subpar work because they know you will swoop in and fix it. They know that if they run late for a deadline, you will stop what you are doing and lend a hand to get it done. Essentially, they are stealing your brainpower, and you are letting them.

Some people are born brain bandits, but the sad truth is that you have helped to create many brain bandits in your life because you let them get away with it. Your drive for perfection and unyielding commitment to meet deadlines has let others around you ease up just a bit.

So how do you turn this around? You have to introduce a language of accountability and make sure that people are clear on expectations and understand the deadlines. You should never directly correct someone else's work. You can provide feedback and edits, but do not handle the cleanup no matter how tempting or no matter how much faster you think you can get it done. There is no shortage of other people who are placing parameters on their work; every now and then you can have permission to do the same.

Of course, this is more difficult when you are in business for yourself or are the head of a company or department, but begin to see when it is happening and work your way out of giving away your brainpower when someone else should be using his or her own.

Remain a team player, remain an innovative contributor, just don't remain as someone else's fallback position when he or she cannot get the job done. And what are all that extra stress and work doing to your already strained brain health? Give the work back to the rightful owner, and save yourself from the bandits.

Energy Marauders

Fuel is everything. Without it you simply can't move. Your energy level is essential to your performance by day and your ability to invest in your future at night. But the energy marauders want to feed on your energy. They want to take you down with them, or they want you to lift them out of their difficulties and life dramas.

The fact is: people are exhausting and negative people are the worst. There you are, minding your own business, and in walks an energy marauder who is a bundle of messed-up emotions and negativity seeking your ear, your empathy, and your validation. When these energy marauders arrive, they bring their low-frequency energy, and that usually slows you down just by being near them. Why do you let marauders get away with this behavior? If you were biking, enjoying the scenic countryside, and someone showed up, set up a roadblock, and made you switch directions so that you were now spending the rest of the day biking uphill, wouldn't you be mad? But often you are too polite to these negative people. You may just listen, thinking they will go away, but you are not paying attention to the damage they are doing on your energy levels. By simply listening and giving them attention, you are encouraging repeat behavior.

A complainer is like a Death Eater because there's a suction of negative energy. You can catch a great attitude from great people. —Barbara Corcoran, *real estate mogul and business expert whose positive attitude carried her from a straight 'D' student to a straight 'A+' success story*

Of course, there is certainly a difference between a friend in need and someone who is seeking to zap your energy. As with time thieves and brain bandits, you must learn how to redirect these people so they are not affecting your journey. Do not worry about being polite because obviously they are not worried about being polite with you.

You can either redirect conversations or figure out a way to tell your energy marauder that you have heard the same complaint, story, or problem multiple times and that, therefore, unless he or she creates some different action, you just cannot lend an ear any more. It will be a tough discussion for both of you but one that will conserve your energy in the long run.

Remember, we all have the same amount of time, but our focused energy sets us apart from others. Don't let someone else take that away from you.

Practical Pirates

The battle cries of the practical pirate are "you cannot do that" and "don't work so hard." Pirates want you to be held to the same limiting beliefs that they hold. They scoff at the people who have more in life than they do. They want rewards, but because the rewards have not come to them, they are sure the rewards won't come to you either. They will tell you that your efforts won't pay off, that you are working too hard, and that you need to have more fun.

Deep inside, pirates don't want you to succeed. This is because of two key reasons: 1) they don't want to be wrong, and 2) they don't want to think that they missed out because they weren't confident enough to follow their own dreams.

If I would have listened to the naysayers, I would still be in the Austrian Alps yodeling. —Arnold Schwarzenegger, thirty-eighth Governor of California, actor, businessman, professional bodybuilder, dreamer who turned into a doer (a very strong doer)

Pirates are full of skepticism and criticism. They condemn and complain about your choices and stand by, waiting to judge your failures or declare your successes as nothing more than good fortune. But pirates can be tricky, and they will choose their words carefully so if quoted they will sound supportive. But you know inside that they do not believe in what you are doing. Let's face it, it is hard enough to believe in yourself when things are going well; it is even harder if the people around you and the people who are supposed to love you see life on different terms.

Practical pirates are dangerous. Don't let their limiting beliefs cover up what you know is right. Do not let them undermine your dreams.

The Best Defense against Opposing Forces

Clarity of vision both consciously and subconsciously is everything while on your bold journey. Attacks against your time, brainpower, energy, and belief systems will cloud your thinking and hold you back. Consider the following actions as a way to block the effects of the thieves, bandits, marauders, and pirates.

- Spend time in solitude
- Establish parameters
- Connect with the best of the best

Time in Solitude

Taking time for yourself will provide multiple benefits. It can serve as a way to replenish energy and rebuild gray matter in your brain. It will allow you to focus on your desires and your vision. When you are alone, you can work to cancel out the negative views put upon you by others. You can focus on what brings you joy and get excited and invested in the future. In our busy world, solitude does not need to be extensive meditation or prayer; it simply needs to be time alone without any noise—no phones, no radio, no computer, no TV. It can be a fresh-air walk, escaping to your car during lunch hour, or taking a moment before the house wakes up or after the house has gone to bed. Steal time for yourself because you are worth it.

Establish Parameters

Be confident that you have permission to take a more active role in your own life. Prioritize how much of yourself you willingly give to others. Invest in the most important relationships and limit or remove toxic or negative situations. Don't wait for circumstances to change on their own; help them along by speaking up, establishing limits, or knowing when to walk away.

Connect with the Best

Something delightful happens as you get older. You begin to identify much more quickly the people you meet whom you want in your life. You will find that you become highly attracted to people and situations that you find pleasing and that exude positive energy because you now know how rare a thing it really is.

On this journey, your goal is to go big and wide in your connections, but for your inner circle, seek out only the best of the best connections. Make sure that you give to them the attention that they truly deserve and that you are willing also to receive the positive encouragement that they will give back to you.

Don't let other people diminish your value, take more from you than they give, or cut short your aspirations.

Takeaways

☐ We all have the same amount of time, but how you choose to use your time on a daily basis will propel you forward.

☐ Protect your enthusiasm from the negativity and self-limiting beliefs of others.

☐ Build an inner circle of positive, energetic people who believe in you and who will encourage you.

15

Go and Achieve Influence

Connections change everything. They improve who we are and what we become. They help us keep our edge and show us where the world is going. Most importantly, a vibrant network can open a lifetime of economic opportunities.

Great things in business are never done by one person. They're done by a team of people. —*Steve Jobs, founder of Apple Computers, innovator and visionary who placed a whole new world in the palm of our hands*

It is amazing to me how distant people can be, but then, within one meaningful, unexpected moment, things can change. Through some unique conversation or shared experience we can become connected and find commonality, and with commonality we gain appreciation and use for one another. Because of this, the human side of business can never be underrated or underestimated.

At the beginning of this book, I shared the three main principles that I wanted you to take away. So as we end it, let me ask you:

1. Do you have a 'WHY' for the purpose behind connecting? Have you been able to see how connecting

must be embraced as an indispensable mission and not just an 'I know I should do it' that you think of every now and then?

2. Do you see the vast possibilities that exist to help you grow your network quickly? Have you realized that you must go deep and wide, that you may need to work your way through a lot of 'moments' to get to your 'must contacts,' and that you have the ability to become a super connector?

3. Do you have more insights into the human side of connecting regarding behaviors you may adopt and behaviors you need to avoid? Do you realize that people who are perceived as easy to work with and are recognized as competent can attract more connections? Are you sure that being authentic, relatable, efficient, and dependable can lead to trust and that trust is the greatest level of influence there is?

My wish for you is that you can have wonderful experiences meeting new people and growing your network, that you can be confident and bold in your exchanges, and that your connections will be there for you when you go to launch a new business, make a sale, or find a new job. Or perhaps your connections will be a great support network to help mold you into a better you or simply uplift you in a time of need.

My wish is that with your brilliant network, **you will achieve influence for a lifetime of career success**.

About the Author

With a career spanning more than thirty years, Allison has traversed the ranks in the corporate and non-profit space, having made her way to the top in a variety of C-suite and senior level leadership roles. She has managed international operations, budgets of over $270 million, and served as a partner and advisor to CEOs and company presidents who have resided on five continents. Today, she is considered a global leader and an influence and empowerment authority who knows firsthand the value of building and leveraging relationships for both personal and organizational success.

Those acquainted with Allison recognize her ease with multi-cultural environments and business situations as a result of her extensive travels and experiences. She has served clients in ninety countries, worked with 'heels on the ground' in over thirty countries, and provided keynote presentations and seminars to audiences in twenty countries (and counting).

Through her work with NGOs, Allison was invited to be a member of the Forbes Non-profit Council. In addition, she has served as a board member for nine non-profits and charities, including a turn as president of the American Marketing Association Chicago. She has earned her Certified Association Executive (CAE) credential from the American Society of Association Executives and her Certified Incentive Specialist (CIS) credential from the Society for Incentive Travel Excellence. In 2013, she began her service as the Executive Director and Chief Staff Executive for Zonta

International, a role which furthered her expertise as a gender equality advocate and champion for women in business. In 2017, she was part of the UNA-USA delegation to the Commission on the Status of Women.

Allison views her success as a reflection of the great professionals she has met along the way who have shared knowledge, extended new opportunities, and even carried her through tough times. In 2016, Allison founded Together at the Top to mentor others who are serious about business and help them attain influence and empowerment. Her book, *Connect to Influence*, represents just one aspect of personal development that will enable individuals to remain relevant and achieve influence, which, in turn, will help facilitate economic opportunities (a.k.a. keep the money flowing) throughout their professional journeys.

Always happy to connect (and to share chocolate!), Ms. Summers can be reached on Twitter @allisonsummers, LinkedIn (www.linkedin.com/in/allisonsummerschicago), or on her webpage: AllisonKSummers.com.

A Note of Gratitude

To my mother, who cautioned that I always needed to be able to care for myself with a paycheck, and to my dad who—by going from a Vietnam vet to a barber to a retail manager to a wine salesman to a realtor to an investment broker—demonstrated that everyone can do more and be more if he just works at it.

To David Bean, my first boss in business and the man who taught me how to shake hands, to wear a navy suit, and that to learn good business I had to go on the road and experience the business.

To Brenda Anderson, who facilitated my transition from corporate to nonprofit and without whom I would have never learned the human side of global business.

And to my children—Evan, Caden, and Jorja—who have grown into wonderful human beings I love to be around.

A Comment about Quotes

The funny thing about quotes is someone else always owns them. It is clear they are someone else's thoughts and ideas, but because they resonate with us, we begin collecting them. We jot them down from presentations we sit through, and we mark books with yellow highlighters and pens. We tear them out of 'Quote of the Day' calendars, search for them on BrainyQuote.com or some other inspirational website, and even retweet and repost them if we think our friends need a dose of wisdom. Some of these quotes I have known for years and had kept them scrawled on random pieces of paper tacked on my bulletin board.

Because of the above, it was tough to determine exactly where many of the quotes in this book originally came from. But I can say this: all the quotes used in this book are cited with great respect.

So to all the inspirational leaders whose words have given us something to think about, I thank you.